OWN YOUR ZONE

OWN YOUR ZONE

MAXIMISING STYLE & SPACE TO WORK & LIVE IN THE MODERN HOME

RUTH MATTHEWS

Hardie Grant

BOOKS

In memory of Doris, my first style inspiration,
and for Ted, my everything

Contents

Introduction

Our homes are our personal havens of happiness, supporting us through life's changes, providing a backdrop to our social and familial rituals and affording us respite and reassurance in challenging times. They evolve with us, and a happy home is one that can transform readily, in sync with our needs. When the Happiness Research Institute published The GoodHome Report in 2019, from a sample of over 13,000 interviewees across Europe, they discovered that our overall happiness is affected more by the homes we live in than our jobs or income. And while our well-being doesn't increase when we inhabit larger spaces, the perception of spaciousness has a big impact on happiness. A fifth of us feel we don't have enough space, regardless of the size of her our home.

Our homes shape our lives; they should feel good to be in and intuitive, but so often they are not built for our changing lives, especially as we now ask more from our homes than ever before – not just to bathe, bed and feed us, but to be an office, a yoga studio, a place of retreat. Many of us feel shoe-horned into a space that feels like it can't accommodate our needs.

This is where zoning comes in. Modern zoning is about building flexibility into rooms and coming up with left-field solutions within a room's four walls that provide the opportunity for easy division or multitasking. A well-zoned home navigates the challenges of multifunctional living and allows us to transition in a way that feels intuitive and efficient. From the home I grew up in, to the one I inhabit now, I have never lived in large spaces, so making use of the footprint available and finding hacks to make the space work harder are long-term obsessions of mine.

Who this book is for

You do not technically need to own your zone for this book to be relevant or useful to you. If you rent your property, you should find just as many easily actionable solutions to creating a zoned space that works for you. We will look at clever tricks with perception of space, such as using rugs to anchor purpose, furniture to divide and paint tricks for increasing flow or enhancing the mood within a space. We will also look at clutter and storage, and the best ways to work with the architecture you cannot change or access to

natural light that cannot be altered. We are not about knocking down walls in this book, but rather adapting a space to best accommodate our needs.

How to use this book

This book is not a manual to be followed to the letter. Instead, you will find much of the book has been assigned to either finding your style or enhancing your zone. Because, while a paint-by-numbers approach may lead to well-functioning zones, none of us want our homes to feel sterile. By looking first at the practicalities of a space, and then at how we represent who we are within it, we will be able to move to actioning our zones in a way that feels natural.

Instead of dealing with the spaces we inhabit according to traditional room titles, areas are approached by their function. You will not find dining rooms, living rooms or bedrooms, but eating areas and places where we unwind or sleep. Each zone has been tackled in this way with a strong focus on well-being. Taking zones by function allows us to address the ways in which a well-zoned home can support us in leading more organised, easily navigable and happy lives.

We will look at how to find inspiration and identify which looks appeal to us on a deeper level. Alongside style inspiration, we will spend some time concentrating on colour, the mood it can create and how we can transform

the enjoyment of our spaces by experimenting with it. We will consider how both mental and physical zoning affects the pattern of our day. Finally, we will look at the ways in which we can enhance our living space, including styling, lighting and considerations of modern sustainability.

I have picked the brains of three inspiring professionals to contribute expert tips within the book. You will find Joa Studholme, Farrow & Ball's Colour Curator, providing expert knowledge on how to use colour in smaller homes (see page 116), surface pattern designer Lizzie Evans, creator of Lizzie for SMUG, offering tips on working and living well from home (see page 155), and architect Lizzie Ruinard, who heads neighbourhood studio, on how to build sustainability into our thinking (see page 180).

I will outline accepted wisdoms from interior design throughout, but these are not to be taken as po-faced diktats – if taking your home in the complete opposite direction from a design rule feels right, well sometimes rules are meant to be broken! Talking of breaking rules, there's something I'd like to tackle before we get to any of our chapters, and that is the way in which the landscape of design can feel to the lay person, like you or me.

Democratising design; why your house is a home, not a magazine

When I started developing a passion for interiors with our first home thirteen years ago, I felt very conscious of what was out of my reach. I read high-end interiors magazines religiously and I was very aware of products labelled 'price on application' that I absolutely coveted but knew were out of my budget. I started my blog, Design Soda, in 2013, with quite a few years of decorating experience behind me, with the view of an outsider looking in. I wanted to talk to people like myself, those who believed it was more than possible to balance high-end tastes with a high-street eye. I was bored of being affronted by magazine articles that told me a £200 dining chair was a bargain – times six, this wasn't too far off my monthly net wage at the time, let alone my budget for design. So I well understand that access and affordability are relative terms.

Since I started working in the interiors field after the birth of my son, I was struck by just how narrow the backgrounds of many in the sector were. In my other day job I would meet many kinds of people, but here there was a visible hegemony within interiors, with design edicts being issued by experts all cut from the same cloth. It made me wonder exactly who defined taste. I wondered if there was a connection between the price of professional courses, which could cost tens of thousands of pounds for a basic diploma, and the dominating accepted wisdom on style. I love looking at interiors magazines, but with the knowledge from having my own home photographed for them that unsightly parts of all our lives are edited out, while new props are brought in. Have you ever wondered where on earth the television is in real homes featured in magazines? I know I have. If you can see the seams of this design illusion, then visual inspiration can be taken exactly as it should be.

I have always been attracted to the disrupters within design, the unique voices that challenge the status quo, and one thing I want you to take away from my book is this – there are no wrong answers in interiors. We all have different styles and what makes my heart sing could turn your stomach. That is fine and differing interpretations of beauty are what give life its sparkle. This book is not a directory aimed at interior design students, but rather a friendly conversation on how you can make your home-work-life balance simpler, more enjoyable and more beautiful.

'Taste breaks out of all rules; as soon as it is pigeon-holed it is dead. It must always renew itself, and be seen in new perspectives. Sometimes it can't be recognised but there is a hidden logic about it ... People should try to invent for themselves, only can something "alive" be tasteful.' Cecil Beaton

Zoning

Zoning / What is zoning?

Few homes have the luxury of dedicated rooms for individual functions; most have rooms that are expected to suit an ambitious myriad of competing demands. Our hard-working homes need to fit a lot in and we would like them to do this easily, stylishly and as intuitively as possible.

We all have an idea of what zoning is, but as a term it can sound a little mean and austere, perhaps a little off-putting. However, when done well, zoning is the greatest of solutions, creating a home that is easy to manoeuvre, rewarding to be in and tailored fully to both our style and lifestyle. It will allow us to balance connection and separation, privacy and sociability.

In this chapter we will not be looking to create a claustrophobic system of rabbit-warren-like partitions, but spaces which speak to purpose while retaining flow. Zoning is not about imposing utilitarian divides upon a space, and as you will see, there is far more nuance between successful zoning. The zoning we will look at will have a keen sense of layout, taking on board how you move around a room, how you enjoy the space and how you can achieve a work-life balance through areas that make transition easy.

Partitions may offer distinction between spaces, concealing what you don't want on view, from formal structures and curtains on tracks, to less intrusive rugs that anchor. Considered zoning assigns each task its own space and keeps it within that space, preventing it from spilling out and maintaining spatial flow and a feeling of connection. Outside of practical necessity, zoning can help us to feel happier, providing easily visible ways to move around a home that supports our productivity while also enabling us to inhabit sanctuary spaces or ones that allow us to socialise without being distracted by our working lives. Well-planned zoning is, I believe, intrinsically linked to well-being.

If traditional homes are zoned by walls and room names, modern zoning is about introducing flexibility into those rooms, and devising innovative solutions that provide the opportunity for easy division or multitasking. The best zoning doesn't draw attention to itself, but seamlessly blends in with the architecture of your home. It does not require a huge footprint to successfully divide and reveal, and can, in fact, look more streamlined in average-sized rooms where space is tight. As we will see, some of the solutions in smaller spaces can be persuasive; for example a shelf used as a desk and painted to blend into the wall colour, or a staircase opened up to create a charming office that is the very opposite of a cave.

Your personality and style will also inform how you create a home that feels good to be in. Zoning for some requires movement and energy, while for others it's the reduction of as much noise as possible to allow a space to feel focused. Zoning within the style school you identify with (see pages 73–91) will look different according to the priorities and ethos of that look, weighting different materials and qualities to achieve spatial separation. Zoning to suit our long-term needs can be done in a way which either feels permanent and therefore more readily visible, or more flexibly with functional solutions hidden. Whichever of these solutions works best for you may feel instinctive, but I hope that by the time you have read through this chapter you will have a keen understanding of what you want to implement and why.

Zoning / Practicalities of zoning

When planning your home design it can be easy to jump immediately to the parts that excite you – the colour palettes, textures, a particular look you have seen and want to recreate. But before you get carried away with the aesthetics, it's important to ground yourself in the practicalities and identify what the people who live in your home need. Knowing who uses your space, and at what times of day, or which functions are non-negotiable priorities and which are desirable, is half the challenge. Well-considered zoning is key to creating spaces that are a natural fit for your lifestyle.

Knowing the times of day your home supports particular functions is especially important, as this will inform how you can build in easy flexibility to accommodate multiple uses at different times of day. Being able to identify your priorities is also important. Do you want a generous entertaining space or a private home office? List all of the activities each space will be used for and weigh the activities you have listed according to priority. By listing these demands in order of importance you will be able to focus on what can be achieved, while also accepting the limits of your space.

I love to socialise and imagine I am the very picture of a domestic goddess when I have friends over. I would like my home to convey this, but homes are for living in, and so in our last home we prioritised space to socialise and relax over having a defined eating space. When we cooked for friends in this south London flat, we would serve food on a coffee table made from an old pallet and sit on cushions on the floor around it. This was a relaxed and intimate way of sharing moments with friends. I'm not sure I felt like a domestic goddess, but I also wasn't constrained by convention with an otherwise redundant dining table.

You will need to interrogate each room in your home. Look at how much natural light there is, and at what times of day. Is this space a morning room or an evening one, and does it work with the light or against it? Question the layout you inherit before assuming it is the optimum. Rather than knocking down walls, investigate whether there are other ways you can make use of the utility of your home. If your bedroom is a good size and it steals the best of the morning light, perhaps it would work better as a home office. If you can easily switch the purpose of a room to maximise the use

of natural light, try it out now before you embark on decoration, only to discover later that your swapped rooms still don't function as well as you would like.

Alongside looking at your architecture to highlight characterful focal points and spending time considering the possibilities of space, there may be off-beat solutions that are not immediately obvious. While examining the bones of your home, identify whether there are there architectural opportunities for storage or zoning. Is there an underused space that could be repurposed to provide a function? For example, a home office positioned on the landing won't intrude on living space and will answer the desire for separateness in the division between labour and sanctuary.

Floor plans

Once you've assessed what you need your home to include you can move to looking at the bones of your space. Measuring each room and planning a scaled-down drawing on graph paper allows you to see many of the practical basics a paid professional will identify for you. To begin with, add the things that can't be easily moved such as windows, doors, radiators, cupboards and plug sockets. Have a long look at the useable space you are left with and identify the room's focal point. Once you add in the furniture – biggest pieces first – is there still activity room?

A golden rule of interior design is to allow 80–100 cm (31–39 inches) of circulation space between functions for movement. These calculations err on the generous side so you don't need to treat this as a hard and fast rule, but does your furniture placement accommodate easy movement within functions connected to the same space? Are there things that can be moved to improve ease of use? Interrogate the choices previous owners have made, if indeed they have made them. Perhaps if a door was rehung to the other side of its frame, or if it opened in a different direction, you would open up a whole new spatial vista. The simple switch of the direction a door opens can have a huge impact. In our house, doing exactly this in the tiny bathroom increased the useable floor size by a staggering 30 per cent. You could also consider replacing the hinged traditional door. Perhaps pocket doors on recessed tracks are the best fit? Or maybe it's bi-folds or even removing the door entirely if the space doesn't rely on privacy.

One of the best practical tips for imagining how furniture will sit in a space is to place paper cut outs, or even cardboard boxes, as a 3-D approximation on the floor where the pieces will be. This is especially helpful if you are struggling to visualise your new space and will help you to avoid costly mistakes. It is particularly helpful in tight spaces where each addition needs to earn its place, or when buying bulkier items.

Zoning / Working with the architecture of your home

One of the ways you can create a home that feels intuitive and easy to use is to work with the architecture you inherit. If you live in an apartment in a row of traditional Victorian terraced houses you will likely have many nooks and crannies that can be utilised for storage or repurposed as useable space. Conversely, if you are living in a new build, you are likely working with a space without character, but that feels more naturally primed for reorganisation. Each of us will have a mixture of opportunities and limitations from the style of building we inhabit.

Period properties

Smaller traditional period homes were not designed for our modern multifunctional demands. If you live in a period home it likely has a drawing room made for entertaining visitors, a dining room for all meals and a kitchen for all scullery activities. If you are lucky, you may have a spare room which can function as a home office, a hobby room, etc. If you work from home, and you have a number of people living in it, from a small family to housemates, you will probably begin to see the fault lines of this. Our sociable spaces now need to work a lot harder – they contain televisions, music players, sofas for lounging, possibly a play area for a small child, or a home office space for an adult, a place to work out and, of course, a sociable space to invite friends into. Our homes were built to be vacant during the working day and to provide retreat and utility in the evenings.

One of the most appealing things about living in a period property is the architectural details that give a home character. If you do live in a period home, you are the custodian of heritage and I would caution you to think carefully before removing any period features. However, sometimes an alteration can not only be necessary, but absolutely desirable, too. Panelled storage is a great example of this – if it is in keeping with the style of your property then it will add to the character, and if it isn't, I still feel it can work in the right space as contrasting old with new can look really beautiful.

Le mur du couloir

Ce mur peut retenir votre attention,
vos idées neuves, votre imperméable,
VOS LIVRES, vos illustrations insolites,
des photos, *VOS OEUVRES*, vos espoirs,
vos trésors et autres objets précieux,
vos médailles, *VOTRE CHAPEAU*,
vos dessins d'enfant, des milliers de notes,
VOS LUMIÈRES, vos interrupteurs,
vos souvenirs, vos succès,
LES TRACES DE VOS RÊVES,
le plan du métro d'ici ou d'ailleurs,
vos patères, *VOTRE ÈCHARPE*,
l'empreinte du temps.

Fabriquée en brique et plâtre;
peinture French Grey pâle.
Hauteur 152cm x largeur 110cm.
La base est habillée d'une plinthe.
Il vous servira toute la vie.

Ce texte est un imitation de be-poles™ pour Merci

If your stairs are positioned in the right spot, and it is permissible under fire regulations, opening up a staircase and completely removing the wall or panels that enclose it can be a really stylish way of grabbing extra floor space from an understairs area that usually houses items which only accumulate dust. With some shelving fixed to the wall and a desk surface underneath, you could have yourself the perfect office space carved out from an area you don't even usually notice.

Make up for lack of floor space in period homes by thinking upwards. Install shelving or cupboards that stretch up to the ceiling. Use a foldable stepladder for items you don't use so much at the top. Looking towards the ceiling, are there other possibilities for storage that could feel less intrusive? A shelf above a door frame can provide the perfect space for a small collection of books or artefacts (non-breakables, please!).

Utilising a bay window

Many of us who inherit a beautiful architectural feature like a bay window don't know what to do with it. But bay windows can often provide extra footprint which is easily utilised. If you have such a window, keep window dressing minimal, installing custom-made shutters, plain roller blinds (shades) and linen curtains. Then you could position a round dining table, or a window seat with built-in cupboards underneath. In my home we have a very small living room with a bay window. After lots of research and measuring, I have a two-seater sofa with a pull-out storage tray housing children's toys and remote controls underneath. The previous owners had nothing here except some storage boxes. It was a dead space, but two sofas in the small room is cosy and they create a focal purpose.

New builds

Homes classed as new builds often get bad press in the design world, levelled with accusations of bad build quality and white-box syndrome. In fact, new builds often offer far more workable spaces. They are designed to maximise their footprint and what you may lack in character you often gain fourfold with useable space. The loss of those nooks and crannies, built for old-fashioned purposes or existing as wasted space, means you don't need to find left-field solutions to maximise your home's square footage. However, like every good adage, what a new build provides on the one hand can highlight what it takes away with the other.

In a newer home you may want to add character, focal points and also junctures so that multifunctional spaces don't feel overwhelming. This could include exaggerating doorways for a broken plan design (see page 34) or using bold colours and wallpapers to create a space that excites and signals your style.

When your home has utilitarian straight lines, there is a world of storage possibilities that you can utilise very effectively. A wall of storage either side of a door can be a great space to hold items, or to display the pieces that make your house feel uniquely yours. If you go one step further and build in a wall of storage to divide a space, then a simple set of pocket doors housed behind one side of your bookcase can be a really effective way of zoning. They will enable you to shut off spaces when you want a quiet or cosy area but also allow your space to be a part of the wider narrative of your home, while gaining valuable natural light.

One of the pitfalls of standard newer builds can be that the rooms feel boxy and square. If this is the case in your home, then circles are your new best friend! A circular table or desk is a great shape to use in your interior. Circles are easy shapes to live with, and they can act as breakers to counteract the feel of 'boxiness'. With a new build you are likely to find storage solutions more intuitive, but you may find that while your storage needs are met, the feeling of homeliness isn't. You may need to concentrate on adding layers to create zones, from large-scale artworks to vintage dressers (hutches) and display shelving. Adding a place of interest for the eye to settle on is the key to creating spaces that feel pleasurable to be in.

NEVER STOP SHOWING SOMEONE
HOW MUCH THEY MEAN TO YOU.

AT SOME POINT YOU JUST
HAVE TO LET GO OF WHAT
YOU THOUGHT SHOULD HAPPEN
AND LIVE IN WHAT IS HAPPENING

Toothpaste
Cinnamon
Fabric Softener
Body moisturiser
Berries
liquitabs
Coffee pods
Porridge

There is a halfway house in zoning which is neither as permanent as built partition or as casual as ad-hoc zoning. This zoning is perfect in larger scale spaces or more open-plan ones, which are often found in new builds. Internal Crittall windows can look very chic in new-build spaces, creating areas that are quiet and enclosed while retaining the feel of light and space that this accommodation offers. If your space feels a little harsh, a plant wall on a trellis can be a beautiful focal point division which also imbues the calmness of nature.

A note on renting

If you are renting, you may need to think a little more outside the box with your zoning solutions. When looking at storage, you will probably need to invest in furniture that is easy to take with you to any future addresses. Where a landlord may not let you paint your space with abandon, or in some cases at all, there are lots of products on the market which you could use to create visual zoning that are temporary. Vinyl wall stickers and removable wallpaper can be a great way of delineating areas on walls and there is a huge variety of styles to suit everyone. If absolutely any pattern, no matter how subtle, is just not you, you could use thick colourful low-tack washi tape or monochrome designs to frame a wall space where your desk will go, or even a particularly striking piece of art that will add focus and definition to different spaces.

Internal Crittall windows can look very chic in new-build spaces, creating areas that are quiet and enclosed while retaining the feel of light and space that this accommodation offers.

Zoning / Open-plan versus broken-plan living

Open-plan

Open plan is a tried and tested solution much loved by architects and homeowners when trying to convert smaller period rooms or integrate new extensions. The attraction of open plan is that it increases natural daylight, which is done by knocking down walls. Our perception of space relies on availability of light to absorb dimensions, and a space that utilises natural light to greatest effect will feel larger, as there are fewer dark corners where space can be filtered and recede.

An open-plan space that is effectively zoned may explain division of task with different kinds of flooring, say kitchen tiles which meet wooden parquetry in a living area. Changes in colour can also signal zones very successfully. However, converting your home to open-plan living will require considerable cost due to the amount of building work involved, and there are certain disadvantages you would want to consider before knocking through rooms with abandon.

In a busy multifunctional space, how do you cut through the noise when everything is laid out in front of you? If you live with housemates or a family and you inhabit your space

for most of the time, open-plan living can leave the inhabitant wondering where they can get away from everyone and all the noise without retreating to the bedroom.

Almost as important a consideration is space lost through the removal of walls. This sounds counterintuitive, doesn't it? But when we knock down walls, we also remove the ability to place things against them, useful things like storage, radiators or large furniture. Yes, you can float a sofa in a room with a credenza backed on to it, but you have lost a great deal of space to store things against on either side of the removed wall. Open-plan living is a popular style when refurbishing a home, and it can undoubtedly provide an incredibly light and airy feel which aids communication between residents, but before you reach for the wrecking ball, consider fully what you gain and what you lose.

Broken plan

A newer solution, becoming more and more popular in recent times, is broken-plan living, which is a hybrid of traditional and open-plan. The broken-plan space marries elements of open plan with a sympathy for enclosure. It can be super effective in smaller multifunctional spaces, allowing things to remain hidden when necessary and to unfold as you navigate around the space, revealing its areas on a natural progression. This approach can mean knocking down a wall to create a double space, or partially removing it. It also commonly means removing a wall and reinstating the division with something less visually intrusive.

Broken plan, while a significant investment, will allow you to enjoy areas of privacy and spaces that clearly delineate purpose without losing views to natural light or across the vista of a property. It is a best-of-both-worlds scenario, particularly if one part of your living space is heavily deprived of natural light.

The kinds of partition you may use here are pretty limitless. You may want to divide space using half or glass partition walls. In new-build homes where you are not encumbered by retaining characterful features you could remove doors and enlarge their gaps to create a connectedness while maintaining privacy. One of the divisions I really love, and which shouldn't cost you the same investment as the others mentioned, are walls of semi-open and open shelving systems. These answer the need for storage and division while also allowing light to filter in from joining spaces.

Using a sofa to create a juncture between where a workspace ends and downtime begins will aid easy transition.

Ad-hoc zoning

There are many stylish ways to zone a space that do not require the same investment as built or fixed solutions and are ideal in a rented property. The arrangement of furniture can be a very useful way to formalise purpose, even within small spaces where no partitioning is possible. Using a sofa to create a juncture between where a workspace ends and downtime begins, or simply arranging furniture around corners of the room for different activities, will aid easy transition and assist with the way you mentally separate and zone.

Freestanding open bookcases and shelving are a great way of zoning, either filled with books and objects to create a solid divide and feeling of permanent separation or left sparser for a more linear and relaxed partitioning. Rugs are a really accessible way of creating zones, visually demarcating a space, say under a dining table or within the seating area of a living space.

Curtains on runners are an elegant answer to zoning which will create focus, free from visual distraction, and versatility, being opened at the end of the working day to re-unify the room.

Zoning / Using paint to partition

A lot of homes come with a downstairs space that is neither fully open plan or traditionally closed. Thanks to a past trend in smaller terraced (row) homes for knocking through living and dining-room dividing walls to create a larger double space, a lot of us will live with these kinds of rooms. They are a really nice halfway measure, allowing us to open up space and perceive vistas and perhaps most crucially maximising the possibility of light, which alters our perception of spaciousness.

Traditionally these spaces have been painted in one blanket colour to enhance the unity of the space. A beautiful way to zone can be simply to paint these rooms as though they were separate spaces using the steel ceiling joist which replaced the dividing wall as the location of the colour divide. Keeping the flooring the same throughout and adding accessories to both sides which mirror the colour of the opposite space will allow you to distinguish each area for different uses while pulling the space together cohesively.

The feature wall

The feature wall is now a part of the modern lexicon of home style, and for good reason. Feature walls allow you to inject a dash of personality through colour or pattern without overwhelming a space. If your home has either a smaller footprint or a lot of use built into it, painting the walls in bright colours or lining them with highly patterned paper can feel jarring, bouncy or discordant, whereas restricting your chosen colour or paper to a contained area or feature wall allows you to express your style through a visual destination. The traditional paint or paper on a fireplace wall is a great way of highlighting architectural features and drawing the eye towards a central characterful statement in the room.

The modern feature wall

There are lots of ways you can incorporate a pop of colour, or several, without following the lines delineated by your building, and you do not need to use a fireplace or alcove to guide you. A very clever way to introduce colour which feels fun, and a tiny bit stylised, is through feature shapes. This could be done with geometric shapes for a playful layering of colour, or with circular scallops and arches. Though the description of these techniques sounds a little like modern trompe l'oeil, the effect is anything but naff. And the best part is that although they look skilful, they require little talent. Some decorator's tape for geometric shapes, with a pencil on string added for arches and a quick search on the internet for instruction, and you are all set to add textural interest to your space.

Half measures

Painting the lower part of just one wall can delineate purpose beautifully or, when painted right around the lower part of a room's walls, create a cohesive feel in a space that has many activities zoned within it. Painting just the bottom section of a wall is a clever way of incorporating bolder or punchier colours since they will recede more than colour at eye level. If there's a colour you are really attracted to, but you're not sure it will work as a complete wash, painting to half height will personalise a space and add drama without the overwhelm.

Zoning / Zone and flow

A house with great flow will feel good to inhabit. It will feel instinctive, but, like all things with good design, some thought goes behind its effortless feel. It's a little like having a signature style with your wardrobe or being an auteur of cinema. If you've watched enough Hitchcock or Tarantino, you will know when you are watching one of their works and the signature hallmarks to look out for. There are talismans hidden in details, but once you know the thought process behind them, you can link the touchstones together.

The way your interior is organised and decorated has an impact on the overall feel of your home, and flow is what makes the dialogue between spaces feel harmonious. It's one of those words that we can all subconsciously translate into our spaces without much thought, but it's also something we should keep as a marker at the back of our minds with each room we plan. A home that flows gently from one room to the next is our aim.

You can have the best storage and zoning in the world, but without flow these two things will never really speak to each other and create harmony. If you set the flow right, your home shouldn't feel awkward. Your signature style could be beige and textural or bold and intricate, but the principles of flow remain the same. Knowing your style and thinking about a collection of rooms holistically rather than in isolation, even if you decorate over time as budget allows, will reward you with a space which is easy and pleasurable to be in.

Imagine your home without doorways. Do all the rooms feel comfortable together? In a big country house this won't matter so much, but in smaller spaces it is really important. So, you don't want to paint every room in the same colour? Who would? Flow finds its harmony through a mixture of cohesion and tension. It is a common misconception that lots of neutrality can create cohesion in a space. While it's true that a minimal backdrop will filter some of the energy of a space, I wouldn't recommend this approach if it isn't your natural style. You may end up living in a very tasteful, cohesive but bland non-space. In other words, something other than yours, not your home.

Echoes and commonality

The Scandinavians have a brilliant phrase which encapsulates much of what we are going to talk about with flow and that is the red thread. In design the red thread is a subtle 'throughline' which connects our spaces together through essential commonality. It does not mean symmetry, and each room of your home can be decorated quite differently, but if your spaces speak to each other, echoing connections of theme, stories and ideas, they have the red thread.

This kind of design thread, or common theme, between connecting spaces, will enhance flow without diminishing personality or style agency. A sense of unity can be achieved with simple echoes, from surfaces to fabrics, that signal a holistic feel in a space. If you are at the start of a total refurb you could choose to have the whole of your ground-floor flooring choices in one material. Or if you are taking a more piecemeal approach to decorating, using the same woods in your furniture choices works very well at subtly bringing all your space into flow.

Think, too, about balance of contrast. Flow is not only expressed through commonality but also by what it chooses to underline. The use of light and dark, rough and smooth, straight and curved, will give your interior life while also highlighting through its juxtaposition where synthesis lies.

Colour and flow

It is worth spending some time thinking about your home's colour palette as this can really define the flow of your spaces. Depending on the number of rooms you have, I would suggest that your palette should be roughly half the number of rooms you have plus two for playing. Once you have chosen your palette you could add flow subtly with accent colours. If you have chosen pink for walls in one room, consider using a little pink in connecting spaces on cushions or accessories.

One persuasive way to add flow and link spaces is to paint all your skirting (base) boards and door frames in the same shade, one which is slightly bolder than standard white. It is fairly easy to update the space when you find yourself drawn to a new shade a few years down the line.

In small rooms that fulfil several purposes it can be especially hard to get the flow right within the space. One strategy could be to paint every surface in the same colour – painting walls, ceiling, skirting (base) boards and even floors in one shade will blur boundaries and increase the feel of space while cutting the disharmony of different functions. This approach will feel more accessible in lighter colours, but in especially compact and light-deprived spaces, if you feel brave enough, a very dark tone can also be really effective at cutting out distractions.

Looking outwards

Don't forget that flow can extend outwards too. How does your home flow with the outside? One trick for extending flow within smaller spaces is to make a connection between outside and in, which will blur and expand boundaries. Whether you use houseplants which reflect the view of your garden, paint walls in natural green shades that mirror the outside or leave windows unadorned to emphasise the view, creating a home in sympathy with its surroundings will make it feel open and outward looking, which will be both grounding and expansive.

Sightlines

To enhance the flow from one area to another, lining up furniture in connected spaces will add weight to the visual journey. If you have a knocked-through space, think about the sightlines through the space as you enter it. Is there anything you can do to guide the eye to connect the space? Perhaps your coffee table should line up with your dining table in an adjoining space.

Flow: The pivotal importance of your hallway

Earlier we imagined how a home would look without doorways. Imagining this scenario, your sightline will probably settle upon an often overlooked and very hardworking part of your home – the entrance hall. You have no doubt thought about how your hallway can answer your practical needs – where shoes and coats go, for example – but how does it feel? Is it obviously a part of your home, rather than an area to be entered and exited rapidly? Whether your hallway is light and grand or narrow and dark, it is an incredibly important part of any interior scheme.

I see hallways as an extension of the kerb-appeal-greeting of your home, anchoring your style, setting the scene, welcoming you home, inviting guests in and, on a practical level, a part of the home you engage with all the time. It is also your connecting view from the rooms you inhabit.

In the hallway you can afford to be a little braver than in other spaces. Although you use it all the time, it is not a space you spend great periods of time in, so it won't irk you (too much!) if you choose something bold and a little out of your comfort zone. While I'm not advising choosing a hallway that feels inauthentic, I am suggesting that you take things up a notch here to increase the joy you feel within the home.

My hallway (shown on pages 52 and 53) has a cocooning and glamorous feel. It doesn't sit quite within the design scheme of the rest of the ground floor, but here is why it works: it holds echoes of things you will find throughout my home, from small details like brass fittings and door numbers which echo door handles and light switch preferences, to larger things which give clues to the style of my home. It is in one of my signature colours and it echoes palette combinations I have used in the rest of my home.

The palette of my home is a mix of neutrals, blues, pinks and greens. While my hallway does not contain a whiff of pink, even in an accessory, it is framed by it. From the muddy pink of my living-room walls, to the quiet pink of my dining-room ceiling extended to the door frame which joins the hallway and then on to our downstairs bathroom, painted in a deeply saturated rose, the echo of pink with green is repeated again and again as you walk through the downstairs of our home. You finally end up in the kitchen, which is painted in a soft grey, echoing back to where you started at the front door, and with the muddy pink living room accented by the same kitchen shade of grey on the ceiling and woodwork. So, the first door surround of my hallway mirrors and leads the eye naturally to my kitchen at the back of the house. Flow is achieved here where our visual journey takes on linked layers without underlining them and in a way that feels natural and without juncture.

The wallpaper nods to my love of natural history, which is evidenced throughout my house; indeed, further down my hallway you will find a collection of vintage framed butterflies. Our storage comprises vintage solutions – an old ruler turned into coat pegs and a vintage shandy crate repurposed as a boot box – and you will find at least one piece of vintage anchoring each room in the house. All these links feel instinctive and this is how flow is created, not by reproducing the exact same thing one room after another but in helping the eye almost imperceptibly to make links between spaces, so that contrasts can work in harmony with the flow of a space.

In my narrow and dark hallway, instead of applying lashings of reflective white paint, I chose a look that was in line with the elegance of the downstairs while also having fun bringing the glamour up a notch. The walls are painted in a deep mid-tone shade of green blue and the space is accented by brass accessories.

Zoning / Maximising the feeling of space

Although you cannot alter the square footage of a space without building an extension, there are many things you can do to increase the impression of space. This isn't Tardis-style magic but there are definite tricks you can use to fool the eye into believing it perceives more space than is physically there.

Using vertical stripes on a wall will emphasise ceiling height, whereas dark tones on flooring will draw the eye down and distract from a low ceiling. Conversely, if you want to increase the feeling of floor space in a room, opting for light floors and painting the walls slightly (or far) darker will open up the vista of the floor.

Natural light is one of your greatest tools for augmenting the feel of space. If your room lacks natural light, using reflective finishes such as glass, metal, acrylic and metallics will boost the feeling of space by helping to bounce what light you do have around the room. Similarly, a well-placed large mirror which reflects a window will increase the perception of space dramatically.

Finding the right fit – furniture and space

Before investing in furniture, ask yourself whether it does more than answer your style brief. Will it also contribute to multifunctionality? We are not all going to be comfortable living with a pull-down bed, but perhaps you don't need matching dining chairs. Can you find chairs that will adapt to other purposes, but can be placed around the table at mealtimes? If you can't find an eclectic mix of chairs that suits this purpose, and you use your dining table to work from, perhaps a set of stackable chairs that can be stored neatly nearby when not in use is your best solution.

Showing a bit of leg

Have you ever lived in a home with woodchip-papered walls? In our last home all walls and ceilings were woodchipped. If you have ever lived in a home like this, you will know that walls recede when these chaotic bumps are removed, allowing the eye to perceive and define boundaries. The same is true of furniture; when you can detect, or even clearly see, space beneath furniture, it looks lighter, and the floor space feels bigger.

An easily recognisable and defining ethos of Mid-Century Scandinavian furniture was design which provided answers to modern dilemmas of function and the utility of space. Virtually every sofa from this period had legs and a silhouette frame. The eponymous Eames folding tables, their British counterparts the Ercol nested tables, minimal wooden-framed sofas – all were built to answer function while remaining light. Unless you have specific inbuilt storage underneath, for example beneath a bed, a piece of heavy furniture really can't earn its keep in a smaller space.

Having lived most of my adult life in apartments with awkwardly shaped rooms and now in a house with a small footprint, one thing I hold as a design deal-breaker is furniture with legs. I absolutely hate the heavy imposing feel of furniture that hides floor space and own hardly any pieces of furniture like this. Happily, my preference has its roots in interior design rules. The more floor space the eye can see, the greater the perception of space. If you are short on space, the majority of your furniture should allow for the floor to be seen beneath.

Trick reflections

One of the absolute best space deceivers in a home is a well-placed oversized mirror. A large mirror over a fireplace will reflect the space back to the eye and appear twice the size as you enter a room. It will also bounce extra light around the room, enhancing the perception of airiness and space. A large rectangular mirror will give you a symmetrical reflection the eye can quickly define. I favour round mirrors as I love how they conceal and reveal, with reflections that create vignettes, illuminating a fractional reflection of space that subverts the eyes' ability to make defining boundaries. Convex mirrors can be lovely in tighter spaces where they will reflect a greater area and magnify the feeling of space.

Zoning / Storage

Moving home is, in theory, the perfect time to address storage to our new location. But it is also one of the most stressful times of life, and in the zeal to unpack and get order in our new space, we often end up hiding a random mess of things in storage behind closed doors. When they aren't objects we use regularly enough, they remain in these jumble cupboards which feel unnavigable.

If this sounds familiar, then before you start thinking about storage grab a notepad and start writing a list of the items you access most frequently. If you do this over a few weeks it should be easy to identify what comes to the top of this list. These are your front pieces, the ones that require easy access. You may find that some of these things group well together and are most suitable for something more ad-hoc, like a stylish storage basket you like keeping on display. Then there will be the pieces that you want to rotate seasonally – blankets for autumn and winter, perhaps. Finally, the items that you barely use, but still need to keep, can be placed furthest back or highest up within your chosen storage.

Storage options

Unless you are especially utilitarian, it's unlikely that you are going to feel happy in a space hemmed in by reams of closed storage. However, a certain amount of built-in storage is essential in most spaces and

especially so in confined ones. Depending on your needs and architecture, you are probably going to need a combination of concealed storage, built in behind doors, and more visible open storage of shelves and baskets. If you have a modern style, then streamlined built-in storage could be practical. Clever minimalist functionality, like press catches on doors and drawers, will help you maintain a sleeker space; you could also build a fold-down desk into your storage, allowing you to maximise multifunctionality and switch zones without visual intrusion.

An entire wall of built-in cupboards is a really practical solution. While you will lose floor space, they are much less visually intrusive than other types of storage. They can also be a great backdrop for styling. Think about what can be placed in front of your storage without interrupting the flow of use. If you are going to use this storage to help you switch your home's function daily, you won't want to place anything cumbersome like a sofa in front of it. But perhaps plants in pots, occasional chairs or a small table in front of cupboards could make the area feel more homely and styled.

Once you have identified the obvious places to fit in the bulk of your storage, it is worth doing a walk-through of your space to seek out hidden corners of unused areas that provide a storage fix. I sometimes think that homes where storage has been built into all nooks and crannies can feel a little mean, but a well-placed shelf above a door or levelled across an alcove or wall will look distinguished.

In my home I have a beautiful sideboard with a reverse inlay patterned front facade. It would traditionally have housed best crockery for dinner parties but is the perfect size to house my DVD collection. Making beautiful pieces truly useful can involve a little extra leg work, but they are worth it for the visual impact gained.

Choose vintage

One option to introduce aesthetics that feel individual to you is to repurpose vintage pieces to make them work in your space. This can be a great way of harnessing storage that doesn't interrupt the flow of your style.

Vintage apothecary chests are great places to store a host of essentials and vintage shop fittings on castors look absolutely incredible in zoned spaces, where they add storage interest and double up as a room divider.

Perhaps a set of pigeonhole drawers are perfect for CDs, or the miscellany of life.

THINGS
I LiKe

HAPPY

A

TINTURA
DE
IPECACUANA

VINO
DE
CONDURANGO

FIGUIER

GARANCE DORÉ

LOVE × STYLE × LIFE

LONG SAFETY
MATCHES

PUM·LAP·P.

MARANT·N.

·R·GENTIAN

POT·BICHR·

Defining Your Style

One of the foundations of impactful design, which both works for the owner and feels good to be in, is a home that can identify its style story. By style story, I don't mean tearsheet looks translated from magazines, but spaces which have evolved to reflect the interests and sensibilities of the people that inhabit them.

Being able to identify the styles that speak to you is really important, so that you don't feel overwhelmed by the plethora of competing choices, especially in tighter spaces which can quickly feel saturated. But, while they will inform your key decisions, you shouldn't feel hemmed-in or bound by styles – a well-chosen wrong piece can create the perfect tension in a space. Using a piece that diverges from the central style-story of a room will add patina and storytelling, while signalling a relaxed environment where the owner is unencumbered by prescriptive design rules.

Sometimes you will have a lightbulb moment that inspires all of the decisions for a space. Other times it will be an amalgamation of things you have acquired over years and which tell your story. Most importantly, you need to feel comfortable in your choices and sure that they work for your space.

It should go without saying that you won't be decorating your space to impress other people, but to enhance your own enjoyment of home. While friends are very kind about my own home, I never decorate for the approval of others – they don't need to live in my home week in week out. But it can be harder to avoid these pitfalls than you may think. Time and again the results come in from home surveys that people are inclined to decorate with an aspirational outlook that impresses others. I want you to feel empowered to make decisions on your own terms, placing the practical considerations of multifunctional living alongside your own style.

Defining Your Style /
Sourcing inspiration

Looking for inspiration can be an open-ended task. There are obvious places you can look – books, magazines, blogs, Instagram, Pinterest, etc. All are great at presenting you with ideas you haven't thought of or come across before, but they can also feel overwhelming. I would recommend looking at these sources and trying to narrow down the elements which have really caught your eye. You don't need to copy, or be literal, in order to be inspired, and you don't need to have a high-end budget to translate the parts of a design that really sing to you. Perhaps you love a Mid-Century kitchen, but it is way out of your budget. Maybe you could learn the DIY skills to install your own plywood cabinet doors.

When you open your eyes, you will find that inspiration is literally everywhere. And when you start to look you almost can't stop seeing! Looking beyond the perimeters of traditional sources of inspiration can lead to a more grounded and relatable home. If you live in a big city, perhaps the styles of architecture, variety of shop displays, the faience tiles of London tube stations, the lines of New York skyscrapers or the clothes people wear on their journeys (how they have paired colours and textures) will inspire you. Or if you live somewhere more remote, perhaps you have chosen a calmer pace of life, maybe the changing seasons are your chief inspiration and a more rustic and biophilic approach (see page 179), bringing the outside in and reflecting your surroundings, is more your style.

'Fashion is a way of not having to decide who you are. Style is deciding who you are and being able to perpetuate it.'

Quentin Crisp

Visual touchstones of cinema

One of the questions I often initially ask clients I work with is which movies they love the style of, as these can be a great place to start an education in interior design. While you won't learn the techniques of layout or placement of lighting, a lot of thought and a huge budget go into set design, which makes excellent wallpaper viewing. Film is incredibly rich in visual cues to inspire. I will often learn some aesthetics from even the most mundane or mediocre movie.

Think about what piques your interest when looking at films. Most of us won't be able to recreate the set of *Metropolis* or *Blade Runner*, but perhaps you love the saturated and stylised movies of Wes Anderson, or the juxtaposition of primary colours with white in some of Godard's classic movies of the 60s. Whether you are seduced by the Art Deco elegance of the hotel in *Top Hat*, Carrie Bradshaw's bohemian brownstone in *Sex and The City*, or the chintzy glory of ornately patterned wallpapers in *Atonement*, movies are there to visually fall in love with, an aspirational smorgasbord with elements that are translatable in small ways in all our homes.

Commercial spaces for magpies

Commercial design can be an invaluable reference tool, not just for inspiration (though give me an original Italian terrazzo hotel lobby any day and I will be happy) but for practical reasons. Hotels, cafes and shops are all designed to get the most bang for their buck in spaces that need to be resilient and hard wearing, while also being alluring and planned to maximise every inch without disrupting the feel. Next time you find yourself in a cafe that you love, pause to look at how each element of its design has been planned. Are you inspired by the surfaces, colours or textures? How have they created their particular ambience? You may find an idea that informs the practical element of your living, such as how the nuts and bolts of furniture, storage and lighting are arranged. It is always useful to have a way of compartmentalising, whether it is visual style or practicality and flow that speak to you with inspirations. This will help you to deconstruct what you see and translate these ideas to your own living space.

A note on trends

The thing about trends is that you can be served up something which feels desirable because it is different, but which may very soon feel uninspired. When decorating our previous home, I started to see brass pineapples before they became a trend. A saved search on eBay turned up the perfect vintage brass pineapple storage pot. Fast forward two years and every piece of glittery pink stationery had pineapples on it! You will see a lot of these trends filter down and become a part of disposable popular culture, in the process becoming removed from the glint of uniqueness in your original discovery. I still have this pineapple, of course I do, I loved it enough to wait several months to find the perfect piece. But my point is this: be prepared for new and emerging trends to come and go, only buy into those that you will love for years to come and don't be seduced by the fickle world of online fads.

Mood boards

Physical sources of inspiration can feel less overwhelming than the inexhaustible stream of online content available. I like to keep a file with wallet leaves full of ideas I've torn from magazines, art exhibition flyers and pamphlets from design shows. They may not speak to me immediately but will hold the kernel of an idea I am inspired by later.

Mood boards, where you have spent time collecting samples of paint, fabric and materials, will help you answer many questions. You will be able to identify quite quickly if your design answers your brief, if it's true to your style, the ambience of the room, if it feels too busy and chaotic, or a little bland and missing tension. Sometimes it can be hard to see these things when they are a series of curated photographs on a board on the screen. A real-life mood board is a really useful way of road testing before committing. Take photos of your mood board on your phone and you will never be more than a glance away from checking if something works when it catches your eye.

Defining Your Style / Style schools
– be your own interior designer

Defining your style isn't as simple as it sounds, and quizzes will rarely give you accurate results. It can be hard to commit to one definition and it sometimes seems to me that it's just this commitment that can feel really intimidating. Nobody wants to spend money on beautiful furnishings that jar in situ. We want to feel confident that when we invest in items for the home they will feel easy and natural within our setting. Knowing your style framework is useful, because, even when you think you have exactly what you need, especially when spending a lot of time perusing home décor, it can be easy to get caught by the lure of an item later regretted.

When thinking about decorating your home it can be useful to know your style as it will help to guide you to a scheme with more cohesion and stop you from veering off track. That's not to say the odd wrong piece can't be just right, but having a basic fluency that underscores your home will make it feel both effortless and good to be in.

Most of us fall within two basic groupings: those who like sleek and modern and those who have a more retrospective approach. That's not to say that this leaning will be extreme or pronounced, but it is likely there. You may not covet either a simple white box or a room with highly patterned wallcoverings, but we will all lean slightly nearer to one side than the other. This, then, is our basic inclination. If you consult your wardrobe, you may find the same is reinforced. Often our clothing can be a good place to look, particularly for confirmation of the colours, patterns and textures that speak to us. You may naturally feel pulled towards several styles. That's fine, most of us are not only one thing, but perhaps you have one central style with two others playing supporting acts.

Moving towards the more official naming of design styles, I will talk about how each style is achieved, hero pieces and the ethos to give you an idea of design recipes for your rooms. I will also provide real life inspirations with both hotels and restaurants from around the world that encapsulate the spirit of the design schools we look at. But do take these recipes with a pinch of salt. Remember: contrast is interesting and totally matchy-matchy spaces feel inhibiting. There are crossovers too. For example, Modern Scandinavian often uses original modernist pieces; conversely, Eclectic Bohemian takes interior pieces from the mid-century but contextualises them among more ornamentation than they would have originally had.

So, which style are you? Have a look through the following pages and think about which most encapsulates your approach. For each look I have included a list of common materials alongside commercial destinations that hold inspiration and cultural resonance to the style.

The unique style of 2LG Studios in their design home, which they describe as joyful minimalism and which could only be theirs.

Mid-Century Modern

If you were a material, you would be wood – stylish, timeless, practical and dependable. You have impeccable taste. Of course you do! This is the most pre-eminent design school of the modern age, encompassing a range of designers from Desert Modernism in America to Scandinavian post-war architects and designers. You are a practical aesthete to the core. Impeccable, stylised, with a keen focus on functionalism, enhancing your living environment to be effortlessly practical and beautiful comes naturally. You are probably attracted to open-plan style living and huge picture windows. Staid, overly ornamental period homes put your design antennae on edge.

Taking its cue from the Bauhaus in the inter-war period, Mid-Century Modern was the post-war rejection of aristocratic flamboyance. As a Mid-Century purist, you dislike unnecessary frills but have an appreciation of streamlined, sculptural and ergonomic shapes. Being particularly drawn to Scandinavian Mid-Century Modernism may be a boon, as many great architects of the movement had a holistic approach to design which encompassed textiles, pattern, glassware and furniture, with many of these classics still in production today. You may be the most likely to interpret zoning needs within an open-plan scheme.

Materials to use:
Warm woods and veneers in
    materials like teak
Sleek silhouetted shapes
Honest metals like brass
    and nickel
Streamlined chandeliers and
    sculptural lighting
Graphic patterns

Sources of inspiration:
Level One, Adelaide
Café Vitória, Porto
Double Standard at The Standard,
    London
Royal Hotel, Copenhagen (where
    everything from the façade to the
carpets and cutlery is designed by
    modernist legend Arne Jacobsen)
The Barbican, London
Frank Lloyd Wright's Fallingwater,
    Pennsylvania
Neighbourhoods of Palm Springs

Rustic

Your abode is all about warmth, comfort, serenity and the feeling of homeliness. Your home is both your personal haven and a warm welcome to your friends. As a design magpie, you have borrowed from Scandinavian and Industrial to update the meaning of the term rustic. You like interiors to feel a little casual and undone, you look for items and materials that have an off-beat beauty and patina. You may use Industrial materials that are unrefined, but they will be blended with soft textures and warming woods for a relaxed, sustainable interior. While not a hardcore minimalist by any stretch, you are likely to decorate in neutral hues or earthy tones. Your home will be textured by layers which make a play of materials – think parquet flooring, Crittall room divides, soft woods and fake fur throws, raw and rough surfaces that feel intentionally unfinished. Whether big or small, your home will always feel cosy and sanctuary-like thanks to the priority placed on small moments of everyday celebration.

Materials to use:
Berber rugs
Herringbone tiles
Raw metals and revealed fixtures
Woods in many types and finishes
Natural materials like rattan and wicker
    to add texture and depth
Natural stone, wood flooring or
    whitewashed floors
Tongue and groove
Metal chairs

Sources of inspiration:
Barchel and Graanmarkt 13, Antwerp
Oaxen Krog, Stockholm
Bourne & Hollingsworth, London
Common, Manchester
Soho Farmhouse, Oxfordshire
Artist Residence, London
Nutchel cabins, Les Ardennes
Masseria Violetta, Puglia

Modern Traditionalist

This look has a quiet sophistication and comfort to it that is informed by elegance and endurance. When you read classic novels, you can imagine yourself inhabiting them, and your style eye is informed by accepted wisdom of aestherics. If this is your style, you have an appreciation of the past but not pastiche, and your personal haven is less likely to be trend driven. Nostalgic, dependable and with an appreciation for the finer things in life, your home nods towards the elegance of a halcyon past. You have probably chosen a home with period features and would not feel comfortable among lots of zany accessories. You are at ease among the refined splendour of city destination hotels and restaurants. When outdoors, you probably gravitate towards scenes of weathered provincial charm or bucolic landscapes. You have a love of luxury with a timeless feel and would prefer to invest in heirloom pieces that won't date with time.

Materials to use:

Wooden shutters

Antique lamps

Persian rugs

Oil portraits

Classic patterns such as
    damask or toile de Jouy

Chandeliers

Dark wood furniture

Parquet

Large statement mirrors

Sources of inspiration:

The Wolseley, London

Caffè Florian, Venice

Beaverbrook Hotel, Surrey

Airelles Gordes, La Bastide

The Ludlow, New York

Maximalist

This look is all about the layers. It is rich and luxe in variety. Homes that are maximalist belong to collectors who display their treasures with abandon. If this is you, your ideal space will be saturated, lively, dramatic, thriving on contrast and definition. You like objects, lots of them, or clashing prints – maybe both. Your home is invigorating and full of inspiration. When you were younger, you may have considered being an individual the most treasured attribute you possessed, and now that you have charge of your own walls this individualism is writ large, with playful abandon. This kind of interior can appear to the casual observer as if the inhabitant doesn't have boundaries, which conversely makes it feel welcoming, but successful maximalist space is keenly thought out and each clash and juxtaposition chosen with care. In a smaller space you may need to rein yourself in so that your home doesn't become a gilded cage of clutter. Perhaps you will limit wallpaper to your eating area, or confine many of your treasures and memories to a display cabinet or shelving unit.

Materials to use:
Saturated and highly patterned wallpaper
Accent-coloured woodwork
Luxurious fabrics like velvet
Encaustic tiles
Neon signs
Metallic- or gloss-painted ceilings
Exotic indoor plants

Sources of inspiration:
The Gallery, Sketch, London
The Lobster Club, New York
Bob Bob Ricard, London
Ave Mario, London
Hôtel Les Deux Gares, Paris
Crosby Street Hotel, New York
Edificio Miami, San Juan
Ovolo, South Yarra

Modern Minimalist

I like your style. I wish I were able to stick within your demandingly beautiful ethos, but I get distracted by too many other more immediate styles. You are tonal, taking your cue from nature through sculptural shapes, natural materials and pigments. You enjoy cutting out the noise of more lively spaces and celebrating simple moments of fika or hygge in the home. You may be more introverted than other styles and prioritise spaces of escape and enclosure within the home, but you have a deep understanding of what is utterly grounded and beautiful. You have softer edges than traditional minimalism, and more than a slight nod towards the traditional Japanese concept of wabi sabi. With an emphasis on pared-back tones, there is a hushed calm to your home, which feels retreat-like. You are disciplined about what you bring into your home, prizing items with longevity and craftsmanship. You probably dress impeccably, understanding the power of understatement. When you visit a new city you search out palm houses in botanical gardens for their sculptural greenery and elegant simplicity. Your harmonious home makes a feature of cosy understatement. This sophisticated, architectural and organised style is ideally suited to smaller homes.

Materials to use:
Light toned woods like birch and oak
Heritage furniture, Scandinavian
    design classics
Glass vases, linen napkins and candles
Easy, natural layers in light or
    monochrome tones
Architectural simplicity with built-in
    storage
Organic shapes
Abstract art work and sculptures
Greenery and foliage

Sources of inspiration:
Época, Porto
Otto, Berlin
Torafuku, Vancouver
No. 19, Melbourne
Miss Clara Hotel, Stockholm
Port Hotel, Eastbourne
Home by Ferm Living, Copenhagen

Eclectic Bohemian

This is a style that is woven through many interior looks, but a bohemian's home highlights things only hinted at by other design themes. You are creative and have a fine understanding of colour. Your style is casual despite a firm appreciation of beauty. You are drawn to layers of storytelling, often through artisan wares and globally sourced pieces. Your home is your canvas, you will swerve anything that feels obvious, preferring a lived-in look that uses pattern and colour without rules. Unlike the Maximalist, contrast is not defined here by deliberate clashes. Your home will look unfinished and be dotted with vintage pieces and finds from your travels, much like your wardrobe. You are happiest sourcing items in flea markets and galleries. Your style is unique and inimitable since it showcases things that hold meaning to you, but it flows in a way that feels easy and not contrived. You may be a bit of an intellectual snob but you won't let on publicly. You love to have company over and your uninhibited home draws parallels to your natural charm with its interest in looking outwards. Living in a smaller space may cause you to be stricter with your possessions than comes naturally, but your space will always feel unique and entirely original.

Materials to use:
Natural lime wash paints
Worn rugs and upholstery
Inlaid furniture
Casual occasional seating in the
    form of ottomans and bean bags
Intricate global patterns

Sources of inspiration:
Paradise by way of Kensal Green,
    London
National Arts Club, New York
Galleon Cafe, Melbourne
Charleston House, Sussex
Goodtime Hotel, Miami Beach
L'hotel Barceló Torre de Madrid, Madrid
Hôtel Panache, Paris

The Disruptor

You are the cool kid, the individual, an outsider most comfortable in design spaces that don't feel safe or expected. You cannot imagine feeling comfortable in the pedestrian mainstream, or in spaces with stifling good taste. You may like to take inspiration from classic styles but you imbue them with your own meanings and irreverence. You are playful and curious and at the cutting edge. If you were fashion you'd be streetwear, all boundary-breaking neon woven trainers and knowing swagger. Your interior finds definition in juxtaposition. You like the freedom from constraints exhibited by the Memphis movement and may draw on areas like graphic design for home decoration. You are the most likely to place kitsch in your home with a big ironic wink attached. Happy out of your comfort zone, you are at ease in a space that pushes boundaries. Your home will be stylised, absolutely awesome and perhaps a little jarring, but you find discord motivating and will thrive in this inspirational space.

Materials to use:
You don't accept rules so I can't provide you with them! You are probably going to rule the world ...

Sources of inspiration:
Bar Luce, Milan
Opasíy Tom restaurant, Warsaw
Cafezal coffee house, Milan
Ladurée Aoyama, Tokyo
Hotel Keyforest, Hokuto
Naumi Studio Hotel, Wellington
La Muralla Roja, Manzanera

Defining Your Style / Colour

It never ceases to amaze me how a carefully chosen colour speaks so much about the decorator's individual energy and personality. Our reaction to colour is unique; we all see colours differently. As Josef Albers demonstrated when questioning his Bauhaus students, even when a shade is suggested that is widely known, such as Coca-Cola red, each person will identify their own unique shade of red as a match.

It's a little like the refrain of that well-known song, 'You say tomato, I say tomato'. We interpret colours differently according to their cultural meaning, our position in the world and personal memories and associations. As a result, we all have very different thresholds for colour. Some will thrive on the bold tones of comic-book primary colours, others retreat within jewel-like dark tones of infinite depth and, for many, the quiet tones of grey or neutrals are the happiest bedfellows.

Changing the colour of an interior space is one of the cheapest and most transformative things you can do in your home. It will change both mood and behaviour, and can be used practically to zone an area, highlight a detail or to blur boundaries. Once you have decorated, a well-chosen shade has the power to take your breath away. In fact, I liken new paint colour to taking a lover. No, really! A new colour in a room can make you feel alive again, and it's likely you won't be able to stop checking in on it for the next week or two, to confirm its charm and perfection. As years go by, it will form a part of your story, informing how you see memories within your home. It's a perfect love story, really. Until you move on to the next shade. Well, this happens to me at least.

The colours we paint our walls can have a striking effect on our psychological outlook: too much blue depresses us, red can make us angry and yellow can give us headaches. But colour also has the power to enhance our lives and our connection to space. When colours we may not be naturally drawn to are introduced in small shots within functional zones they can either motivate or calm us.

Colour and our perception of it is altered by environment and there are lots of practical tips that can help you decide on which shades to choose. In rooms with northern light, soft greys will feel more successful than whites, which can take on a dingy cast with the light. Rooms that are south facing will absorb colour to a greater degree, making chosen shades appear lighter. The position of colour can be as important as the shade itself. A bold colour on the walls of the rooms where you spend much of your time will feel very different to a less used space. Living areas that are well used often benefit from softer shades, but areas you spend less time in like bathrooms, hallways and inside cupboards can often be a brilliant space to dare to follow your bolder colour inclinations.

Colour not only transforms our feeling within a space, it can also be a practical tool, helping us to conceal or punctuate, to add either harmony or tension. It can help us to hide things we dislike. Using one uniform shade on all surfaces, for example, stops us from reading boundaries and will allow an ugly element to recede. Recessive colours, in cooler light tones, pull away from the eye and will impact our perception of the size of a room, making it seem bigger, while warm bold and dominating colours will have a friendly enveloping effect that draws the eye in. Using a bold colour on an accent can create impact by cutting through wishy-washy spaces that otherwise feel numb or sterile.

Layering lighter and darker tones of the same colour will always look chic and sophisticated, but be careful of mixing different hues of the same tone as these can cause real discord. Having an idea of the main colour palette of your home will give it a better rhythm and flow, so do take some time to consider the psychological merits of each of the shades we will be exploring.

'As "gentlemen prefer blondes", so everyone has preference for certain colours and prejudices against others. This applies to colour combinations as well ... usually a special effort in using disliked colours ends with our falling in love with them.' Josef Albers

Blue

Blue is a primary colour that feels very pure, conjuring images of nature and serenity. It is a colour that is linked to the divine, at times more precious as an artist's material than gold, and it is read by the eye with one of the greatest of intensities. From elegant watery blues to calm aquamarines, and inky night-sky-navy, blue is a colour you will find all around you in nature, and perhaps because of this it is a colour we are very comfortable with.

Blue looks particularly striking in bohemian homes as it can be decadent, escapist and bold. Step forward the peacock blues of the Bloomsbury Set, and the eponymously named Yves Klein Blue. The most beautiful of mid-blues often owe a debt of gratitude to both grey and green and they can be very comfortable, almost whispered, colours to live with. A muted blue is the perfect shade for dipping your toe in the water without feeling too bold.

Psychologically, strong blues aid focused thought, while light blues have a calming effect on the mind. It is a shade suited to workspaces, an intellectual shade, aiding clarity of thought. It is also serene, producing calming chemicals that help us cut through clutter and distractions to focus on what's important. Blue is the colour that reflects the circadian rhythms, conjuring images of the sea and skies in the clement weather of daytime, or reminding us of night skies in the evening and turning thoughts naturally towards unwinding. It is a colour that is highly affected by the light and changes with it; it can take on an opalescent quality. In its greatest intensity it is best suited to the sunniest rooms.

A great accent in a white space, blue will add vibrancy and heighten energy when placed in juxtaposition to white. If the coolness of blue concerns you, a touch of green will stop blue from feeling cold. Green used on skirting (base) boards and woodwork is a beautiful colour combination with blue walls, which emphasises the hinterland between the two colours while reflecting nature's most dominant tones.

Green

From paradise to evil, green is a colour that has produced diverse reactions and interpretations throughout human history. An earth tone, a gentle legend, green is nature's great stress reliever. It is also surely the colour of the 21st century, chosen three times in the last decade by Pantone as their colour of the year. Green feels like a very modern shade wedded to both environmentalism and the desire to reconnect with nature.

Green is one of the more versatile shades, and can feel scholarly or elegant, sociable or quiet depending on the shade used. There are energetic hues like olive through to peaceful sages and the coolest of all, where an injection of black cancels out the warmth of yellow to produce deep forest greens which can be absolutely hypnotic on a wall. The versatility of green means that we have many cultural associations with it, from the austerity of sludge green to the decadence and poison of absinthe and arsenic. While there are shades that sound jaunty – as in British Racing Green – in the main, green is considered a colour of restoration and of gentle movement within nature. It is also a colour that represents growth. Think of the phrase 'new and a little green' to symbolise youthful inexperience and enthusiasm for growth.

Green is often interpreted in more pastoral terms, connected to stillness and reflection, rejuvenation and serenity. It is the central colour of Biophilia (see page 179). Even the introduction of green through plants within a space will calm us.

Like blue, green is perfect in an office for aiding productivity and clear thinking. It looks gorgeous with warmer accents such as wood and brass. It is also a wonderfully sociable colour in an eating space or living room. In gardens and bouquets there is nothing fresher or more interesting than green paired with white. Black is also a great foil to sage green and a winning combination if you want to underline the secret warmth green can produce.

Red

The hottest of the warm shades, red meets the eye head on. As the first colour the human eye perceives, it always appears nearer than it is. It symbolises dynamism and confidence, inextricably linked to blood and power. It also lends meaning to the passions, being a colour of carnality, romance and the devil. Red is the amphetamine of the colour wheel, it stimulates, raises heart rate and can make us impatient. But it can invigorate us too, imbuing spaces with a defiant optimism and warm energy.

Red spaces feel hotter than others and so will increase our perception of heat. Red also signals danger, and it can make small spaces feel oppressive. But it's not all bad news, as in the right space red will provide warmth and excitement. Small injections of red aid concentration and a red trim on the wall by your desk can be a really effective way of motivating alertness.

Neon red is a shade made for the bold, and if you have the gumption it can be the most stunning of all. As any woman who has tried to find the perfect shade of red lipstick will know, no two vivid reds are the same. Scarlet can be pillar-box, infused with blue or with an orange vein.

For reasons of its strength and intensity, red is an exceptional minor player. I love to use earthier, slightly blackened reds like burgundy or merlot as accents in my schemes. These tones can look wonderful when paired with pinks, tans, taupes and black. If a space feels empty and clinical, an accent of red will fill the void, drawing the eye towards its warmth and energy. Taking ourselves back to film school for inspiration, Jean-Luc Godard is an exceptional director for illustrating the power of bright primary red against stark white. Dirty reds look perfect among baby blues, ramping up the sophistication of a space and allowing it to feel more saturated.

Pink

Pink for all its connotations of femininity, tenderness and prettiness has not always been seen this way. Before it was wedded to feminine domesticity, it was seen in relation to its primary parent – red, a colour of power and monarchy. Pink is a soothing shade; like rose-tinted glasses, it makes the world feel friendlier. From blush pastel pinks to dirtier woodier roses, pink is a physically soothing, enveloping antidote colour which rebalances time spent on blue light technology.

At some point in the first decade of the 21st century the term 'millennial pink' was coined to describe the vast array of items, aimed chiefly but not exclusively at women, appearing in a modern colour that combined rose pink with a touch of peach. Today pink endures. It is too warm, too forgiving and too easy a shade to live with not to have earned its long-term place among the popular hues. One of the colours I am most asked about in my own home is a very muddy pink that we have in our living room (see page 158). This shade, thanks to its heavy dose of brown, feels grown-up, something enduring, timeless and pleasing on the eye.

A classically romantic shade, pink can feel rebellious too. Sorbet pinks reminiscent of David Hockney's California paintings mixed with punchy reds can be beautiful in quite an unexpected way. A hit of red will really ramp up the impact of other more innocent shades, turning colours that could be saccharine into something far more arresting (see page 101).. Pink is certainly also political; whether along gender lines or sexuality, it is a colour that is constantly being redefined. Using a retro shade of pink can be done perceptively. Modern adopters of this shade reframe nostalgic ideological associations by using pink to recontextualise its meanings for modern eyes.

Pink can also be fun, a way of signalling that you don't have a serious approach to your home. It is very versatile, lending itself to many colour combinations. It will look fresh and crisp when paired with white, elegant and sophisticated with grey and I love the compliment of a really dark shade against pink – black especially will add seriousness and a layer of drama. But pink can work equally well with more vibrant shades. A hit of bright orange among pink can add energy to a space that needs more life.

Yellow

Yellow is a very emotional colour, an optimistic one that people associate with the colour of the sun. But yellow is not in fact the colour of the sun. This is one of many untruths in our cultural interpretation of colour. However, it is certainly true that yellow is associated with our feelings of warmth on a bright sunny day. Yellow occupies a wide spectrum in interiors from bright and bold canary yellow to deeper sunflower and mustard, and more muted shades like clay through to common neutrals like magnolia. Yellow is believed to enhance creativity and self-esteem; it is also the colour of yellow-bellied cowardice.

If you find the lack of light in winter months difficult to endure, yellow may be a good choice within your palette, particularly in dark rooms where it will mirror the effect of sunlight. Traditionally the colour of morning rooms, yellow is invigorating since it energises us and encourages confidence. However, you should also be a little cautious of an abundance of yellow as it can overstimulate the nervous system and is not ideal in spaces where you want to switch off.

Yellow is a confident, rebellious, somewhat attention-seeking shade. A bohemian colour, full of the confidence of subversion, it informs the title of the infamous British literary digest *The Yellow Book*, edited by Aubrey Beardsley, surely the most synonymously decadent artist of his age. Bohemian yellows are not the colour of lemons or sunshine, but of deeper, more autumnal yellows, nearer to mustard and ochre. They work well in rooms where you want to add drama without removing light. A strong yellow will always look gorgeous when paired with a shade of teal. Yellow is a colour common to Mid-Century design thanks to the heavy use of oak and beech in modernist furniture.

Happily, if you don't feel brave enough to take on an abundance of yellow, and many of us don't, then introducing small injections of it can produce the same mood-boosting effects, say on a sofa or splash-back tiles. Even in singular doses, as a vase of daffodils, achillea or mimosa, yellow is a colour that can bring positive vibes to a space.

Orange

Orange is the extrovert of the colour wheel, a colour of visibility, vibrancy and fun. In an interior it will add verve and make a scheme feel spontaneous and independent. It is also a hugely sociable colour, imbuing an atmosphere with positivity and encouraging people to open up to each other, making it a great colour for communication and connection. Since its heavy use in the 70s, orange has remained rather unfashionable in the subsequent decades. It is almost singularly absent from interiors, aside from retro schemes.

Orange is fresh and vibrant; it is almost always bright. In nature you will find it most commonly on its namesake fruit, in the water on fish and coral, on autumn leaves and across the Australian outback. It is also, to come back to our discussion of yellow on page 105, the true shade of the sun. The tequila sunrise cocktail, with its mix of orange and grenadine, is a far nearer approximation of the sun than painted pictures hanging up to dry in nursery schools and kindergartens.

Orange cannot help but be a colour of invigoration; its zingy hue is both rejuvenating and exciting. It is also hugely motivating. Having an area of orange around you when you are learning a new skill is helpful as the colour aids assimilation and makes you more open to new ideas. Leaving aside neon oranges, there are a few more muted, and perhaps more useable, varieties of orange. Peach, coral, terracotta, rust and tan all have the sun-baked base of orange with a grounding weight of either dirty red or dark yellow. Coincidentally, if we are happy to accept peach as a shade of orange, the millennial pink shade discussed on page 102 owes a large debt to peach for its popularity.

Orange paired with its complementary colour, blue, always looks good, but especially in the contrast of bright orange with navy. Two shades of orange that work really well together but do not demand the same visual urgency as true orange are peach and rust. This combination feels like a more sophisticated appreciation of pink or red tones, highlighting the link between orange and adjacent colours on the colour wheel.

Black

Black is chic, it is the colour of fashion and solemnity. It is serious too, the classic colour of text for rigorous thinking. If this book had been printed with pastel pink text, I wonder if it would be considered fluffier, less serious or just more difficult to read?

Black, like white, is a non-colour. It reflects the least light of all hues and for this reason has often been classically dismissed as a shade with little use on interior walls. But to dismiss black is egregious. It is a great colour for adding drama, and also completely unrivalled for its ability to make art and objects pop. Beginning with the trend for singular chalkboard walls in family homes, black has evolved in recent years to evoke sophisticated spaces. This is in no small part due to interior designer Abigail Ahern, who's penchant for darkside decorating spawned a legion of followers and popularised the mainstream daubing of inky shades with abandon. Black will look effective as a backdrop to brights, neons and metallics. Think pop art-derivative objects and copper hardware. It signals individualism unencumbered by rules. But there's no avoiding the fact that in the wrong space it can feel cold and intimidating, solemn and depressing.

There are some spaces where traditional wisdom on black has been eschewed. If you have a small room that lacks light, traditional thought leads you to light colours, but black can feel really infinite and also cocooning. Painting walls and ceilings black actually feels expansive since it is harder to read where the space begins or ends. In the right space black adds a quality and definition no other shade can match. It may not feel good if a room is already cold, but if your area lacks both light and space no amount of light paint will change your perception of this, so you may as well go wild and create a truly opulent dark space.

Black is often used as an accent colour, and there is surely no combination considered more chic than the classic monochrome juxtaposition of black and white. A space with white walls will deal really well with a punch of black on the flooring. It is also a great colour for paint hacks – a lick of black paint on UPVC doors or window surrounds (primed first with a suitable specialist primer) can change the whole feel of a room from basic to chic. So long as you are aware of how black will suit your personality and lifestyle, it really isn't a colour to be intimidated by.

White

White, like black, is not technically a colour but a pigment, and it has the most enduring popularity within interiors. Pure white is actually unusual in paint, although it is available. When we think of white paint, we may think of brilliant white, which has blue undertones, or off-white, which has a yellower base. In Sweden a common term for the perfect white that mixes subtle yellows and greys is known as Stockholm White.

White is the colour of cleanliness, impossibly so. If you have ever purchased a white cushion or white clothing you will know that nothing stays white for long. Or if you have painted floorboards white you will be aware of its power to sit in constant defiant judgement, chasting passers-by daily with the dirt that accumulates atop its imperious purity.

White is both unassuming and virtuous. It is medicinal – from doctors' white coats to strait jackets and cells, it has a self-medicating quality that cuts through emotional noise. It is the colour of stillness and looks particularly well in interiors that are sparser, making a play of negative space and contributing a feeling of calm. White, just like black, is a brilliant base colour which will allow decorative objects to come to the fore. A word of caution, though – white can sometimes be too much, and if used on all surfaces and materials it can feel incredibly boring. Take the fashion for the shabby chic style of design which upcycled antique or vintage finds in a blanket of white paint. What began as an inventive way of modernising old objects was soon adopted by others to become a great whitewashing of the past. If you are going to use white on walls and floors, please do not also paint your antiques!

White reflects light, so if you have a small room that gets lots of natural light then white is the shade to use to increase the feeling of space and openness.

Beige

Beige gets a really hard time these days, seen as a non-colour, one that requires less commitment than others, dull even. It's a tone that won't offend anyone, but also isn't likely to ignite great passion either. A default tone, thanks to its unobtrusive and grounded attributes, it has an enduring popularity. Beige is always present, evolving with changing tastes, but the essence remains the same. It feels like the more grown-up older sister to white.

Over the last three decades it has evolved several times, from magnolia with an injection of yellow, to mushroom with a smattering of brown, to the modern-day greige which keeps the muddiness of brown and adds some grey in for good measure. This most recent reinvention of beige has been made to look really chic by our Scandinavians design sisters, and it is currently climbing in popularity to become one of the dominant shades of choice.

Beige is both soft and accommodating. It is very well suited to the layered look, offering some of the warmth of brown with the freshness of white. A romantic tone, from clay to dusty bone, beige blends well with vintage and rough wood for tension. It can be very chic too – think of walls with a fresh layer of natural toned tadelakt – it has an aura which is naturally soothing and calm. A beige scheme can look beautiful when other layers of the same tone are used for textural storytelling. Think of marble, natural wool and ceramics juxtaposed with natural linen, a beige on the wall with an alabaster lamp. Beige is comfort food, and a scheme that incorporates this shade will be imbued with a softness and stability that is quiet, steady and relaxing.

Grey

If the last decade had been a colour in interiors, it would have been grey. Grey has been everywhere and it has become shorthand for understated good taste. It's a strange trend when looked at through the lens of colour psychology, suffering from accusations that grey in the home will either drain or depress you. While it is true that grey can make a room feel colder and even smaller, it is a very liveable shade, which almost certainly explains its popularity.

Grey will feel very different according to the background colours mixed into its black and white base, whether it is quietly suggested in dove greys and those nearest to off-white, or punchily pronounced in the darkest of charcoal tones, which have a heavier shot of black added. Architectural greys sit on the bluer spectrum, while cosier greys add the warmth of pink or brown to their base. Grey is as much about its undertones than a simple consideration of black mixed with white. From blue to brown, pink to red and green, there are as many types of grey as there are colours, and they will all feel very different. It is worth looking through the colours we have identified so far to work out which grey base is most in line with your tastes.

Using colour with
Joa Studholme

**Joa Studholme is Head Colour Consultant
at heritage paint brand Farrow & Ball.
She is an author and the developer of the
signature shades many of us now have in
our homes.**

**On approach to colour palette in small
multifunctional spaces and zoning with colour**
While we are spending more time in our
homes, it has become increasingly important
to zone spaces into light bright areas we work
in and darker moodier spaces that we retire
to at night to relax, mimicking the cycle of
natural daylight. Upbeat inspiring colours like
Babouche will boost your creativity and can be
used inside a cupboard to create a desk area,
while rich warm tones like Pelt, when painted in
bookcases or behind shelves, can help to make
a warm cosy space. Colour is the very best way
to zone areas that are used in different ways,
and this switch from light to deep colour helps
to define the end of our working day.

**On the best ways to show your colour
personality without overwhelming small spaces**
Without doubt it is best to start with stronger
tones in smaller areas or rooms you don't use
all the time. Use a bolder tone of a colour you
love in a spare room or in your hallway (which
you are always just passing through so can
afford to be stronger) so that all the rooms off
it feel bigger and lighter. And always remember
to introduce darker tones in darker areas while
keeping your light areas just that – light. There
is no point in trying to fight nature or the light
that you have been given.

On maintaining flow and accent colours

The best way is to use the same colour on all your woodwork and ceilings – this still gives you opportunity to use lots of lovely colour! Think of the sightlines from one space to another and how the colours will affect each other. If you have a very strong colour in a bedroom next to a delicately coloured room, then you will probably lose the flow – it's not about the colour itself, but about the depth of colour.

Accent colours can be introduced in a myriad ways – my current favourite is the use of yellow in window reveals to create a constantly sunny atmosphere in a room.

On where to concentrate more dramatic colours

Start small and in places that are not too prominent. Introduce stronger tones in the back of bookcases or kitchen dressers (my top tip is to cut card that fits between the shelves, and paint that so you can change these areas on a whim – particularly from season to season). And remember that strong colour below your eyeline is much easier to cope with, so go mad on table legs, the underside of baths and kitchen islands!

On switching moods with colour that reflects light

Many of the Farrow & Ball colours with their mysterious underlying black have the propensity to change both colour and mood at different times of day. Light Blue can be clean and upbeat during the day but becomes delightfully silvery as the light fades. Oval Room Blue also feels more serious and greyer in low light than it will in bright sunshine and is a great colour to use in a kitchen you want to turn into an entertaining space at the end of the day.

On creating interest within a blank functional space

If you want to maintain a functional space without introducing colour, look no further than using a combination of finishes. The combination of a Full Gloss on the bottom third of the wall with super-flat Estate Emulsion above it (all in the same colour and with no dado/chair rail) is super exciting. And I am a great believer in using Full Gloss on ceilings (again, in the wall colour) which will bounce any available light around and create interest without it being too prominent.

Defining Your Zone

Working from home has never been more common than it is now. Whether you freelance in a creative field, fit your work around a childcare juggle or were shoehorned into a home office by lockdown or a stay-at-home order, the opportunities and drawbacks of working from home have been brought into sharp focus.

How do you navigate the new work-life balance when your office is at the centre of your sanctuary from the world? What if, like many of us, the size of your home doesn't allow for a dedicated office space? And how do you plan an office area that feels comfortable and productive, good to be in, without impacting on the areas of downtime your home supports?

In this chapter we are going to look at the mental ways we zone our home. We will plan your space and discuss obstacles, providing you with a toolkit to plan your own office space. When you have considered both pitfalls and routines, you should feel set to create a space which utilises the area you have allocated efficiently and which doesn't impact on the flow of your home adversely. We are also going to talk about gearing up, switching off and well-being, looking at the practical steps that answer both mental needs and healthy behaviours. We all have different personality types with varying influencing traits, from procrastination and distraction to the disciplined. If you live with housemates, a communal space can be too sociable for some but enlivening for others.

Do you already have a space that you are using for your home office? How is it working? I have worked in traditional settings, on location and part-time from home for several years. To some extent, the type of work you do will dictate what kind of space you need. You may be completely desk bound or a bit of a free traveller, as I am, who likes to work from several spaces for different tasks. I can be flexible in my movements as my role is varied and I need little more than a laptop, a pencil case and access to a quiet uninterrupted space to function efficiently. But there are some central rules which remain the same for almost everyone.

Defining Your Zone /
Getting in the zone

So many things change when you work from home, and for all the positives, you can find yourself missing the most banal things. The traditional routine of shower-breakfast-commute can counterintuitively be thrown out of kilter by the extra time you gain by working from home. There can be something a little casual about it, you don't necessarily need to be dressed formally, to some extent you can probably plan your time and motivation more flexibly, and you will no longer be pushing yourself onto a packed transport system.

There's an awful lot in favour of being able to work from the comfort of your home. And yet, a challenge that can feel almost as great as switching off is the one of starting your day right, of arriving at your desk at your most dynamic, even when that is only moving from one room to another. We are so used to being relaxed in our dwellings that it can be hard to feel professional, and when we work from home it can be equally difficult to switch off with such ready access to files and emails. How do you signal to your brain that you are switching zones within the same setting without the lines becoming horribly blurred?

Starting the day right

We all have different prompts that we find motivating. For some it's early morning stretches and yoga, while others require a quiet, contemplative space in which to come to in the morning. Most of us will find that our most productive hours are in the morning, and that when we first wake, we are somewhere in between being able to work well and in the sleep zone.

This is the time to either do something nice that sets you up for the day ahead or to remove one of the simple stresses from the day. It could be that you live near a lido or wild swimming location and that the cold blast of water along with exercise invigorates you in the morning. But there are lots of low-key ways to get in the zone too. Most weekday mornings I do the school run, which gives me a simple 20-minute walk outdoors and resets my system.

Tidy home, tidy mind

If one of the chief benefits of working from home is having agency over how your workspace looks and feels, then making sure your workspace is enjoyable and that you actually want to work in it is pivotal. Many of us find it difficult to work in messy spaces, even if we are just passing through them. A quick 20 minutes tidying is worth the time taken before you start your working day to prevent you from losing time being distracted or unfocused.

Feeling professional

For some people the routine of putting on skincare can be a mindful way of starting the day right. Having a space for the things you need on a dressing table or an area in the bedroom or bathroom is integral to the morning routine and having suitable ways of storing or displaying these daily products should be built into your design brief. This is especially valid if you are using a table in your bedroom to work from, as you will need both easy access and the easy ability to stow things away. You have probably heard the advice that you should wear smart clothes and do your hair and make-up if this is something you have traditionally done in your working life. I agree with this up to a point, but something simpler which works for me is to leave my shoes on when I come back in from school drop-off. If you are someone who loves to throw your shoes off the minute you get home in order to relax, what you signal to yourself is that time without shoes is your time.

Tailoring the working day

We all have particular and unique ways that make us work more dynamically from home. It is important to spend some time observing how you function best and planning your routine for getting into the zone accordingly. Alongside getting into a work mindset, you could spend some time tailoring your actual day too; perhaps you benefit from 5–10-minute breathers every hour instead of a traditional tea break or moving around your home to stop you from feeling sedentary. Maybe a head-clearing walk is something you'd like to fit into your routine which will make you feel more dynamic during the working day.

Defining Your Zone /
The home office

Your home office can be tailored to suit your unique preferences (as well as your work requirements), allowing you to control both the aesthetics and ambience of your setting. For this reason, it can be a place where you feel happier and more comfortable than the traditional workplace setting.

Access to natural light is the first and most important consideration in knowing where to locate your office space. Ideally, you should place your desk under the natural light of the window. This will aid concentration and a view to the outside world will act as a buffer to mental function. Perhaps this isn't possible in your own set-up – maybe access to a pretty window view has been prioritised in other functions of your home. But an area with some natural light is desirable, even when this means utilising space meant for a different purpose.

The energy of your space

When creating a space to work from home, you will need to consider the answers to a few basic questions. Do you thrive creatively or cerebrally in lively atmospheres, or need the hush of stillness to concentrate? If you find stimulus energising, you may benefit from incorporating a piece of art with kinetic energy or abstract movement above your desk. Having considered the section on colours in the previous chapter, you probably have an idea of the shades you may want to use in a workspace. A small injection of colour on one wall or trim, in a shade designed to aid concentration or motivation, can have an impact beyond the aesthetics. If you are somebody who finds it hard to concentrate in a white box, and who needs subtle noise from colour, then a stronger toned colour could be your solution.

Perhaps you concentrate better in austere spaces, ones free from clutter, with colours that feel academic. I favour deep greens for office areas, as to me they feel calming and reflective, mirroring the outside world while also echoing serenity and seriousness. But perhaps a deep earthy red does this for you?

The desk

The home office desk, unconfined by the standard office fit, is perhaps the most important decision in creating your home office, though some would argue a comfortable chair just has the edge. You will know the chair that feels comfortable and offers support, but the right desk can be trickier. When choosing a desk I would err towards simpler pieces with narrower dimensions, especially when you don't want it to encroach into your living space outside of office hours. A traditional bureau can be a nice vintage find, but it is likely to be on the bulkier side. If you are looking for a fold-down desk attached to the wall which also feels sturdy it's hard to fault a Murphy desk, and there are many variations available. You could paint the folded-back cover to match the walls so that it blends seamlessly when not in use, or even make a feature of it with some textural wallpaper in a style that matches your look.

A vintage piece is often the perfect fit, providing an aesthetic you are drawn to, while frequently answering practical necessity since many vintage pieces were designed to smaller specifications. Don't forget that there are also pieces of furniture designed for a different use which can be repurposed, a console table for example. As long as you can find a piece that works for practical purposes, you could turn your desk space into one that really inspires you. For more than a decade I have worked from a cheap 1940s desk I bought second-hand. It is an entirely utilitarian wood veneer piece; I have painted the frame in a sludgy French grey and covered the top with an architectural landscape wallpaper by Fornasetti which is protected by a simple sheet of glass cut to size. This desk feels very personal to me and my home style.

If you work from your bedroom, you may find a slimline vintage dressing table, with drawers for storage, will add character to the room. The key to a desk you really want to work from is to find the piece that speaks to both comfort and aesthetics.

One of the great challenges of working within multifunctional small-space living is the juggle between creating a dedicated space to work and one which doesn't intrude into your downtime. Just as you may not want to work from the kitchen table for fear that stacks of dirty dishes and housework distract you, you also don't want to see tomorrow's tasks, or the uncompleted pile of work, when you are trying to unwind and recharge. Even when you can't create a dedicated room for an office, there are ways in which you can achieve separation. It can be an area that can be shut away, or at least be prettified when not in use. I love Scandinavian modular open shelving – once you have configured them to accommodate your work needs, the units can be styled up to look really interesting and since they are slimline, they won't intrude. A simple shelf desk built into this shelving will blend into the background easily while still feeling like your office space when you use it.

Perhaps one end of your dining table is near to a window and natural daylight. If you have a table surface that can expand, say a dining table with drop leaves, you can create a compact desk space in the daytime which can be expanded for dining in the evening. Perhaps you can fit a corner desk behind your sofa and still have room for movement. There are lots of different options for desks on the market and they are no longer only built on grand scales for dedicated spaces. Keeping your work tools as streamlined as possible will also have a big impact when space is tight, so try to find as many wireless tech solutions as you can so that all those wires don't look messy.

The closet office

There are so many creative ways you can incorporate a workspace that remains separate but doesn't require its own room in the modern home, and nowhere is this more ingenious than the cloffice – closet office. If you have a closet space, as the example from 2LG beautifully illustrates opposite, or can use an alcove to create one, then the cloffice could provide a pragmatic solution.

Starting with the worktop for your desk, you need to fix a shelf at the correct desk height (70–76 cm/27½–30 inches from the floor). Adding a separate shelf of the same dimensions underneath on runners will allow you to pull your desk space out and provide a surface for your keyboard if your closet isn't deep enough to accommodate this on the worktop that holds your desktop.

Once you have your worktop planned, look at how much storage you need and can accommodate without overwhelming the space. Keeping your shelving fairly minimal, especially if you are not intending to create a pull-out space, will give you a calmer, more streamlined space to work productively. But don't overlook the opportunity a concealed office space can offer if you have had to rein in your style choices in other areas of your home. A cloffice is ripe ground to really express your individuality with a wow design, as long as you bear in mind it is your workspace too. The most effective cloffices go bold with colour on the interior walls. If you identified a bolder shade in the section on colour (see pages 93–114) which stimulates the most useful mood for your working habits, this is the place to express it.

Some period homes have enviable nooks that once served a purpose but are now redundant. If you have a pantry space that joins another room, this could be an ideal office space. A simple curtain hung on a rail acting as the space divide and providing the opportunity to be shut off when the curtain is redrawn will allow controlled dialogue between your office and other spaces. If you have an alcove, one solution which answers the brief of separation could be to fit a sliding door which can be pulled across to shut off your home office at the end of the day.

The bedroom office

If you work from your bedroom, you will need to think about how you are best able to integrate this. A desk that can be hidden away after use is ideal for allowing you to separate functions. Thinking back to architectural opportunities, if a sliding door isn't practical in your space, an alcove or a wardrobe hidden behind stylish doors when not in use could provide a useful solution.

If you have a dressing table in your bedroom, this is likely placed by natural light. A piece of furniture used for a specific purpose that can be repurposed at other times, maximising access to light throughout the day, offers a great solution in busy spaces.

Having a desk in the bedroom full-time is something that many of us have had to grapple with since working from home became 'the new normal', particularly if you share your home with family or housemates with similar work demands. Your bedroom can provide the best solution since it's often the most peaceful and undisturbed place in the house. However, it can lead to a horrible blurring of boundaries when for half the day you are productive and at your most alert in this space, and then expected to shut out the working world and unwind in the evenings. During working hours it is important to have your back to the bed so that you are not teased by the comfort of pillows and blankets for a nap.

It is also paramount that you are on top of storage for work things. A collection of boxes which can be pushed under the desk or bed at the end of the day, or an ottoman at the end of the bed to house work necessities, are key to your work not intruding when you shut down.

Space to break out

I find break-out zones really important during the working day. This spot should act as a palette cleanser when you hit a lull in productivity during the day. It may go against all the rules of healthy versatile living, but even a zone usually associated with the temptation to nap or watch tv can be a useful break-out spot if you are able to disassociate the two activities.

Defining Your Zone / Play: Switching zones and switching off

When Virginia Woolf delivered her feminist polemic *A Room of One's Own* nearly a hundred years ago, she proposed that women needed both financial autonomy and their own room in order to bloom creatively. The nub of this is the need for a space unencumbered by other people or demands, in which one can allow one's mind the agency to create (and of course, this need applies across all genders).

You may share your home with a busy family, housemates, a partner, or your whole space may be your own. But either way, we all need a space in which we can unwind untethered by people or distractions, a place that allows us to be still. This could be a window seat with a view that doubles as a reading nook. A corner where you work out or meditate. Perhaps it's a quiet area where you can paint and listen to music. Your bedroom could be your sanctuary. What does well-being in the home mean to you?

When you are living and working in the same space, think about how this could support well-being. If you work from home, you may well have already found strategies and learnt the hard way that checking your emails in the small hours, perhaps from different time zones, is never going to set you up well for the day ahead. We ask so much of our homes these days, and ourselves, but do we always centre our well-being within these tasks?

It is incredibly easy to get distracted towards the end of the day, switching into downtime temporarily, perhaps to take a phone call or make dinner for your child, and then resume work in the evening to catch up where you left off. This juggle really takes its toll on our mind's ability to perceive when it needs to be active and when it can recuperate and revive.

Working from home may mean that you do not get the social interaction you thrive on, it may mean not leaving your own four walls for very long periods, feeling akin to a period of convalescence, or it may leave you feeling permanently switched on and unable to sleep. We will talk about sleep on page 148 – after all, it is one of your home's central functions – but first I'd like to talk about that switch at the end of the day and how you use it.

Workouts

Whether it be yoga or Pilates, weight training or aerobics, exercise is brilliant for signalling the end to the working day, allowing you to burn off the troubles of the day or nervous energy and boost your mood at the same time. And it's one of the simplest things to accommodate.

The basics most of us require for home fitness is mood and privacy from family or housemates, and ideally a window with a view. A lot of gym kit is eminently portable. The wall space behind the bedroom door is an ideal spot to locate hooks to hang either equipment or a gym bag so that they are always easy to grab, or if you have a lot of gear a small trolley on wheels can be a stylish way to house equipment when not in use. Even bulkier pieces which most compact homes would have trouble accommodating can now be purchased for multifunctional spaces, such as foldable treadmills which can be stored under your sofa and easily transported for use.

If you are looking to make more of a focal point of the area you work out in, vintage sports equipment can look stunning on the wall – think racquets, skipping ropes, boxing gloves, etc. Or you could create a space in your bedroom that is easily sectioned off by a curtain or screen, with access to a full-length mirror for toning or yoga.

The reading nook

A reading nook is an ever-present staple of the modern interior, and for good reason. Reading is a solitary act which marks our separation from both people and situation, and it is of course possible to be engrossed in a book anywhere. But there's no denying a comfy seat, set apart from the throng of daily life, with light from a window or access to a lamp in the evenings, turned slightly away from elements of distraction in a room, is one of life's little luxuries, a cosy invitation to switch off and disconnect.

You do not need an abundance of space for a nook, it could simply be a chair in front of an alcove bookcase or chest of drawers. If you are serious about the importance of this zone and have space for it, there is nothing more charming than a window seat where you can lounge with a book and unwind.

Eating areas

The feeling of home can be found in its rituals of celebration. Nowhere is this truer than the space where we eat. Many of us probably eat many breakfasts and lunches on the hoof, or at our desks. But most of us probably also value our evening meal as a daily ritual that divides our working day from our time of relaxation. It is a space we really like to be in. Think of Scandinavian hygge, where the focus is less on the food and more on the comfort and conviviality of sharing your day with a partner, family, housemates or friends, creating connection and support. The dining room as a dedicated space is a bit of an anathema in modern times, but we can all create an ambience that feels welcoming and add a little atmosphere that makes us want to linger longer in our dining space.

Your dining table may double up as a workspace. It could be a table or a breakfast bar in the kitchen, or even a low-level coffee table with cushions on the floor. Wherever you eat your evening meal, there are ways in which you can enhance the space while also defining it as a separate location. To start with the basics, think about how you are going to zone your dining area. This could be done with a rug placed under the table which separates the space. It will feel cosy and inviting and from a practical standpoint it will protect hard flooring from chairs pulled back and forth.

You could also zone with your lighting. Pendants at staggered heights give a feel of occasion. Lights over a table anchor the space, and when you attach your lights to long flexes that can be hooked from the ceiling into several positions, at varying heights or more centrally, you will build in versatility for other functions too. Lights on a dimmer switch can be useful here, especially if you work from your dining table, allowing you to bring the light up for working hours and then to recede for relaxation.

Ideally you want to be able to have a dining space which can be cordoned off from other more mundane functions of a room, so that they do not encroach on your downtime. If you have the luxury of a table that is mainly used for eating, there are some really unique uses of paint on ceilings that delineate and zone the area. A dark shade may sound frightening and reminiscent of a floating chasm, but it can provide an opulent cosiness, especially when other elements around the table play to the feeling of cohesion.

If you haven't yet bought a table and are planning to, consider the proportion that is the best fit for the space. If your eating space needs to double as your workspace, there are stylish and cleverly designed tables with extending leaves which can be opened to half or full distance. Furthermore, some of these tables have built storage into the central folding point of the table, perfect for hiding your office paraphernalia. My preference would be to choose a round table as this will help to open up a tighter space while allowing more flexibility in setting. Furniture with slim legs or silhouetted shapes work well in smaller areas, as do materials like glass or acrylic.

What is often referred to as the pinch point in interiors can be very pronounced in dining areas. The pinch point here accounts for space between your dining chairs and the nearest wall – ideally this should be 70-100 cm (27½–39 inches). While this may only be a dream in spaces with smaller footprints, it's important to bear in mind when buying furniture, as no-one wants to feel trapped by a table.

Chairs and seating

And what about the accompanying chairs? One of the cheapest ways of furnishing a dining table is to have mismatched chairs. A mixture of high-street finds in different styles and colours can look really arresting, with the added benefit that some could be stackable, and others set to different purposes around the house when not in use.

But if you want a matching set of chairs that doesn't break the bank, vintage is a great solution. They may require a little effort to paint, varnish or recover to suit your room, but will save you more than a pretty penny from your budget. In our dining room, I bought a set of six 50s stackable plywood chairs for a steal from a furniture clearance dealer. A simpler refurb has given us exactly the relaxed Mid-Century feel we wanted. One of my favourite space-saving styles is fold-up vintage cinema seats which can be wall-hung or placed against the wall next to your dining table, which will provide extra seating without intruding into a space when not in use.

Creating atmosphere

Little things can add to the ambience of an evening meal; we eat with our eyes, after all. I would always invest in some good quality tableware and a candlestick. Unlike vases, where you need several to allow for different varieties of flowers, your home only really needs one well-chosen candleholder. The use of candlelight at the table creates a lovely intimacy, mimicking its use from bygone eras of more formal dining, and bringing a layer of ritual to your table space.

You could choose something simple which feels perfect for light spring evenings but can be made more occasional by adding a few sprigs of greenery in a garland shape. Or you could choose a modular candle that is also an investment piece. We have three Stoff Nagel triptych candleholders in plated silver (there are other materials and I have seen configurations of many more). As they are modular, they are an excellent choice for those acquiring décor over time. These candleholders have been in production for more than fifty years, so there will always be the possibility to add to your collection over time. In our own home, our simple set of three can be configured into many different shapes and so always feels fresh to use.

Bathing

Bathrooms are where you ready yourself for the challenges of the day, and where you wash away your day in the evening. The rituals of cleansing and bathing are essential to well-being and the bathroom is the ultimate sanctuary space, so it would seem remiss not to talk a little about it.

If you are living in a smaller property, the chances are you don't have the biggest bathroom. But when a bathroom is executed successfully it can be space of retreat, solitude and sanctuary, regardless of size.

If you are planning a bathroom makeover or renovation, careful consideration of mood and purpose should inform your background thinking. As always, how the space is used is the first consideration, especially in relation to pay-off between purpose and size – there's little point in housing a bath in a smaller space if no-one ever uses it. Does your bathroom need to uplift you in the morning or relax you in the evening? Perhaps it has a duality of purpose. Secondly, planning in decent storage is key. To maximise the feeling of space in smaller bathrooms you could opt for wall-hung units to provide an illusion of space. There are lots of charming options for mirrored cabinets which provide the dual-purpose of bouncing light around while acting as the mirror.

We've talked about the direction a door is hung before, but it is super important in a bathroom where the square footage can be like a postage stamp. If you have the space in your hallway to hang the door outwards this is the simplest of tricks; if not, a sliding door is a really good solution, though more costly.

It can be hard to find interesting options for bathroom suites and hardware – you will need to be quite determined and creative to find options that feel luxurious but don't come with a high price tag. If you are looking for the sanctuary feel, avoid something that feels too clinical. Off-the-peg suites can feel very sterile, so if you are looking at basic suites consider other places you could bring in warmth, perhaps with wood panelling on walls. Mixing up your grains can also be a nice way of adding warmth and definition with any more uniform elements of your suite. Finally, if you are looking for a peaceful space that will help you to unwind at the end of the day, don't overlook the power of plants to bring calm, or a simple change of paint colour.

Defining Your Zone /
Getting in the zone for sleep

If you have ever been through a period of broken sleep patterns, then you understand the modern malady of tiredness. The working world is no longer set for the majority by the circadian rhythms of tilling the fields. And with a great number of sedentary jobs in the knowledge economy, we have moved from being governed by the hours of natural daylight, hard work and recuperation, to one where technology has made it hard to switch off, and where being stretched and busy is a marker of success, not pity.

Tiredness sounds casual, like an unfortunate by-product of modern life, but long-term tiredness can lead to neurological problems, burnout, and even in the immediate make us unable to connect and listen to others, to be present in our relationships. Beyond this, it will impair our ability to process information and knocks our decision-making power. So how can we create an environment that supports our ability to sleep?

Sleeping space

While we have been discussing well-being, we have been naturally moving towards the room in the house most keenly designed to aid this. As humans we thrive on routine. From school bells announcing playtime through to the traditional clocking-in card at work, routine is intrinsic to the pattern of our lives, and yet it is an aspect that can easily get lost within the interior walls of our home. Aside from the essentials of a well-designed bedroom, getting in the zone for sleep requires being strict about your evening routine. It may seem boring, but setting regular hours is crucial so that your body can learn when it's time to wind down. Building relaxing ceremonies into your downtime routine and sticking to them daily will help the pathways of your brain to recharge and renew ahead of a good night's sleep.

The bedroom can be the ultimate space of safe haven and retreat, a serene room to feel rested in and an escape from the outside world. The two main functions of your bedroom, if it doesn't also double up as a workspace on occasion, is to sleep and to dress. You will need your bedroom to set you up for the day and to

soothe you to sleep without distraction. So, it is logical that these two functions will be at the forefront of your mind when planning the space. First, you may look at how your bedroom feels. If you have got it right, the first word you hit upon will likely be comfort. If you can also say that it feels luxurious and makes a ritual out of relaxation, then go straight to the top of the class! The bedroom needs to be the room in your home that feels most calm; it should be as cosy and comfortable as your living room area.

Bedrooms should be as uncluttered and streamlined as possible, dedicated to the easy reach of your essentials and not clouded by a fog of decorative pieces. You will need a bedside table (nightstand); ones with drawers for overflow storage are my preference. Keep items to a minimum on your bedside so that it is easy to find the things you need for unwinding.

When you sit up in bed, what do you see first? Where your sightline falls is where your eyes will focus with each new day, perhaps it is an art print that inspires you, a view of nature from the window, or a shelf displaying a collection of objects that charms you. Whatever the view, it's an important one to consider, as an inhibitive or invasive view of a wardrobe (closet) stacked with burgeoning clutter atop is not the first thing any of us needs to see on a fresh new day.

You will need lighting that you can dim in the evenings for switching off, while also providing a good light source for getting ready on dark winter mornings when there is no natural light. One of the best space-saving solutions is to have directional wall lamps by your bed which can be focused down in the evenings but swung towards your dressing area in the morning.

Bedrooms can be one of the worst spaces for clutter to build up and nowhere more so than the 'chairdrobe' which holds either clean washing or a full capsule of items not quite ready for the wash – that cardigan you need as an extra layer, a few belts for different jeans; there must be a couple of items out in your room right now in this category. You don't need to make a confessional of them, and unless you are a machine, it's unlikely that your bedroom will be completely clutter free. But equally, nobody wants to see a mounting dump of other daily clutter as they are trying to switch off, so as you walk into your bedroom consider what you can see. If you can see a great many things, it may be time to pare back to add a daily storage section to your cupboards.

Your bed is an obvious focal point and one which you are unlikely to change with trends. But just as important as your bed is your mattress. Two statistics that always surprise me are that the average person spends thirty years of their life sleeping, and yet is more likely to change their car, and even their home, more regularly than their mattress. The comfort of a mattress is often our first thought when assessing our rating of hotel rooms we may spend only a night or two in, but our own mattress doesn't always merit the same interest. A slightly unexciting purchase it may be, but a good mattress is not an area to dismiss.

Next, you should think about your bedroom's supporting textiles. One or two cushions that have the right amount of squish and can be used when you want to sit for longer periods of time in bed, and a well-chosen throw for the colder months. If you have wooden floors, a rug to welcome your feet as you get out of bed is always desirable. Bed linen is also an important part of the experience of your bedroom – natural materials are more breathable and are nicer to sleep on. Cotton has always been popular, but in recent years linen covers have become a bedroom go-to in interior design. There are a few key attributes of linen that make it very well suited to bedding. Linen is a sustainable choice which will get softer with age, it is suited to the more un-done look and never requires ironing. Linen keeps you cooler; this is essential in summer, but being a touch cooler than the room will help you to sleep better all year round. I like to add blankets or throws where necessary to my linen and do not swap out duvets seasonally anymore, which frees up under-bed storage.

One final thought on a bedroom's function as support to well-being: phones. Phones are central to the function of modern life, and yet they can also be the worst culprit in depriving us of sleep. Detaching ourselves from our phones in the evening is something most of us could get better at. A busy multifunctional space needs conscious mental zoning to avoid overstimulation and leaving your phone at the door is crucial to this.

At Home with
Lizzie Evans

Lizzie Evans is a surface pattern designer and creative entrepreneur. She creates a pattern collection of products, is a coach to design-led businesses and a podcaster and has built a reputation around her eye for beautifully curated and interesting aesthetics. Lizzie lives and works from an art deco apartment in north London which she shares with her husband, son and Mabel the cat.

On routines for getting into the zone for work
It's an important part of my working day to actually connect with how I feel, what I want and need and what would feel good. I also really benefit from journaling and will often take a minute to write about how I want to feel that day. It's a great way of connecting with my real and true priorities, as opposed to how I think I 'should' be spending my time.

On multifunctional living
In terms of the set-up of the apartment, my studio is also my living room and it's my favourite room in the flat right now. My desk is very neat in size but also in design. It's an early 20th-century dressing table from a first-class state room on a luxury ship liner, so it's beautiful but also really streamlined and doesn't look like a big clunky desk in the middle of the room. It manages to be the perfect dimensions for me when I'm working at it and has lots of storage for my materials, but it also sits happily and neatly in the room without making a big impact or taking over the space. This makes it easy for the room to have dual usage and in the evenings we chill happily in there without thinking about work.

On creating interest in a compact home
We've collected lots of little and large bits that we love over the years and it brings me great pleasure to curate them around our home. My biggest tip is investing in the

right shelving. We have a mix of Vitsoe, vintage Tomado, Ferm Living, HAY and some other little shelves we've bought at markets or even found left out on the street. Finding the right shelves for your space is half the battle.

On adding colour and texture

I am passionate about deliberately stopping to look and notice what I feel works best. Taking the time to really look and tweak what you're styling until the curation feels right sounds obvious, but being extra intentional is super impactful. I'm as interested in the space left empty around things as I am in the things themselves, so a lot is about finding a balance that my eyes find aesthetically pleasing.

On home décor to enhance creativity

I don't think I would know how to separate the two. The things I love and want to have in my home very much connect with my love of design and designing myself. My home is filled with other people's work that inspires me and therefore makes me feel creative. It's a chicken-and-egg thing.

On switching off

I'm pretty good at switching off in the evenings. Doing dinner and bedtime with my son creates a nice routine for all of us and marks the end of my working day.

On nature and the home

Even as a born and bred city girl, getting lots of light and connecting with nature as part of my working day is really important to me. I have recently moved my desk from the bedroom to the living room and it has been a huge success both for my creativity and mental health. I'm now working in a much larger room, but it's the light and the view that's made the biggest impact.

Another upside of living on top of Clissold Park (and having a three-year-old) is that we get out for walks and fresh air regularly. I find that however productive I feel I can be if I'm at my desk for long periods of time, I always benefit creatively as well as physically from going out for fresh air and a run around.

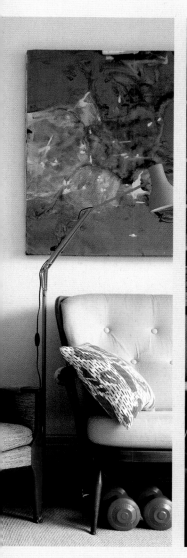

Enhancing Your Zone

Our brains are subconsciously decoding information from our surroundings all the time, and we are all environmentally sensitive to a greater or lesser degree. The smallest of details can have the greatest impact, far more than you may think.

When I rented my first home with my partner, I felt a terrible culture shock on settling in. It was a small studio apartment in a large Victorian villa, with a bed space that looked out onto one of south London's busiest roads to one side and views over a private woodland to the other. I had wanted to live in something characterful and was happy to trade in space for elegance and a location near to amenities. During the first few days of moving in, I had placed a considerable number of personal artefacts, more than perhaps the space naturally allowed, around the home. But still a feeling of unease remained.

And then a sudden change happened when I added some artwork to the walls. You may think it was acclimatisation to my new environment, but it was simpler than that, and something that felt a little pathetic at the time. Outside of the things I couldn't control – the magnolia walls and blue curtains – it was the placement of images that held meaning to us that made me able to view this space as home.

Looking towards why I felt this way, I can see now that I was articulating the powerful connection between the small details of our interior environment and our ability to feel at home. If the home is a tapestry, then the small details which may not be perceptible to others are the threads that hold together how you feel within your space. And I don't just mean art, I mean lighting, hardware and textiles, too. They are all of themselves small details, but ones which can have a huge impact.

In this chapter we are going to turn our gaze towards these small details, then we will look at treating the home more holistically, looking past our zones at how we can build the ethos of well-being and sustainability into them.

'Details are not the details.
They make the design.'
Charles Eames

Enhancing Your Zone / Lighting

Choosing lighting for the home is one of the most basic and non-negotiable of all the decisions you will make. Good lighting is not an afterthought but a building block that mood is created from. It will harness shadow for contrast and without it a space would appear flat and uninviting. And yet, past the central pendant light, knowledge of how lighting can be most usefully and beautifully purposed can feel an intimidating topic.

There are five basic types of lighting and each room in your home should have a mix of several to provide flexibility. Light can alter how we perceive aspects of a room – uplighters directed at ceilings make rooms feel taller, while light targeted at walls will increase the perception of space in a room.

Central statement lighting

Central lights are one of the first things you notice in a room and they are a great place to draw attention to a beautiful light fixture. In certain rooms, chandeliers or other layered centrepiece lights can add a finishing swag to a scheme. While most of us inherit a central light, it should never be your only light source. In practical terms it will light up your space, but often harshly so, and the shadows it creates can leave compact rooms looking much smaller.

Ambient lighting

This is where lighting gets sexy. It's the mood lighting you encounter in restaurants and bars, lighting that feels good to be in and coincidentally that flatters you. Friends will always thank you for ambient lighting as it provides illumination without glare. Adding a feeling of cosiness, ambient lighting should consist of layers of combined light. It is the perfect type of light to use when watching television or working from a screen in the evening.

Task lighting

Task lighting should be directed towards spaces with a purpose – the paperwork on a desk you work from or a place where you read. Task lighting can lead the way in a narrow hallway or help you to see well enough to enjoy a craft in the evening. It should never be focused directly at your eyeline but turned towards the task it is illuminating. Spotlights are an example of task lighting taken from commercial design and were once very popular in homes, but unless recessed they can drown a space with too much light.

Wall lights, uplights and downlights

If you are not in the enviable position of building your own home, extending it or considerably renovating it, some kinds of lighting can be practically, and financially, prohibitive to install. Wall lights may sound like an easy piece for an electrician to tack onto your main lighting system but will ruin even a semi-finished space if investigatory holes are needed to find the source of connection. If wall lights are not an option in your home, there are many stylish uplighters and downlighters you can connect by plug socket and fix to the wall with a couple of screws which will provide the same ambient function. Slim uplit floor lamps are another great option, which in smaller spaces can be tucked behind furniture or in corners of the room, and are great solutions in rental properties.

Dimming the light

It is not always possible to have dimmer switches. But there are other ways you can reduce the glare of central lighting, such as smart light systems which will change LED light-bulbs-settings from warm to white via pressing a remote-control button. Or if you are feeling very low-fi, and you have enough natural light, you could use low watt or filament bulbs for a warmer glow from your main lights.

Enhancing Your Zone / Styling your zone

Working on a wide variety of styling jobs over the last decade, from design festival installations and brand brochures to interiors shoots and residential clients, I have picked up a lot of tips on how things are presented and concealed. But the most useful thing, which I come to time and again, is the placement of objects and the rules which work to make them look best. These are my three golden rules.

1. Contrast and scale

Contrast is the first key to interiors display. Through the tension of heights, materials and variety in the style of objects, you will be able to create something that is both layered and feels pulled together. The smooth glass of a vase next to the rough texture of unfinished earthenware ceramics, the glint of a metal contrasted by wood, or a vintage piece amongst the smooth lines of modern objects all become more interesting than the sum of their parts when placed in contrast. If your collection is all of one type, you can display variety through height. In fact, height is incredibly important to all displays. The use of taller pieces at either end of a display will create visual bookmarks and tension preventing a collection from looking flat, enticing the eye to wander.

2. Negative space

For your objects to look curated they need negative space around them to breathe. It can be very tempting to start filling shelves with everything we find interesting, but this leads to a display feeling chaotic, difficult to read and failing to balance the fine line between interest and a personal junk yard. In the same way you approach clutter and storage, you should curate your objects so that only those items you really love are given centre stage.

3. The rule of odd numbers

This rule states that any collection you display should not make a symmetrical whole. Symmetry is far less interesting to read. Even if you have two symmetrical pieces, you will need to add contrast for the cohesion and tension to sing. Odd numbers are your answer. Think of bookends: they work visually because they are contrasted by a different material, books in between, which makes them a collection of three, an odd number.

Textiles

Using fabric in interiors is a great way to inject an illustration of your personal style, while adding textures that are both visual and sensory. In small spaces, something as simple as a detailed print on a chair or a highly textured rug can help to pull focus and draw the eye to where comfort is suggested. It will also bring a room to life, the interplay of contrasts adding depth and comfort. The transitioning seasons can be reflected by a staple stock of rotational textiles, carefully chosen to suit climate and purpose. I don't simply mean swapping heavy throws in winter for light linens in summer, but also altering your colour and pattern choices too. I tend to use more acid tones in summer and muted ones for autumn. Winter often means monotones to me and spring suggests pastels. Changing up elements of a colour palette is a great way to keep your home feeling fresh, and if you choose standard sized cushions for rotation they require little storage, since it is only the covers you will swap out and store.

As with many other things mentioned in this book, I have a preference for natural materials over manmade, but that does not mean these pieces need to have a high price tag. If you were to invest your money in textiles, you may consider a central rug, something that really sings to you and will change the feel of all furniture around it. Perhaps there will be one textile in the room that is more special than the others, your centrepiece item, which really opens up the tactile possibilities of the space. In the bedroom this will be your duvet cover, which is similar to paint in its transformative effect on space. Whether you chose a pattern or a plain linen which will allow you to change the feel with cushions, buying the odd textile piece above your usual price point is entirely justified when it is a true heirloom piece which you can see the craft behind, and in smaller spaces a showstopper piece can really earn its place among your scheme.

Hardware

You interact with the hardware in your home every day and good hardware is absolutely worth investing in. A well-designed light switch will have similar thought put into the design behind it as a luxury lipstick which is ergonomic to touch and has that satisfying click on closure. Aesthetically, hardware is the finishing trim on a parcel, the piece of velvet ribbon which takes your wrapped item from presentable to a little luxury. Your door handles and light switches, power sockets and the way your tap (faucet) feels and looks – these pieces will all have an impact far beyond their weight in isolation. They are essential pieces of the jigsaw puzzle which contribute to an ambience of elevated luxury.

Curating alternative sources of art

One of the elements a lot of us find hard in home decoration is choosing what to place on our walls. In a lot of ways this feels like the most personal of decisions, and yet, perhaps thanks to the religiously hushed solemnity of art galleries, what we choose to display on our walls can also feel quite public, a declaration of authenticity, style, ethos, humour or sensitivity. I am a firm believer that you should only have on your walls things that really speak to you. Whether you choose to display abstract minimal lines or a huge piece of kitsch, it's your walls, your rules. I love the idea of slightly more unexpected items on walls, providing interest, and often at a fraction of the cost of traditional art. Sourcing art outside of print makers can help you to create an interior which reflects your character and which will inspire.

Stylish freebies

If you visit galleries and exhibitions, they can be brilliant hunting grounds for pieces to hang on your walls. A lot of thought goes into advertising particular exhibitions, stylistically translating their aura, and pieces collected from this pool can feel a lot less cut-and-paste than direct reprints by famous artists. One of my favourite pieces in our home is an A3 paper place mat advertising an exhibition I loved at the Barbican (pictured left), found in their café.

Treasured plates

Hanging plates on walls can be a great addition if your taste is eclectic or retro. You may have found yourself drawn to singular plates over the years, pieces which don't match any sets you have and which were bought purely for aesthetic pleasure. These are the plates you will love seeing on your walls.

Handmade abstracts

Another way of adding interest that feels unique is to create something yourself. We are not all blessed with an artist's precision, but creating abstract pieces or block-printing paint samples onto a piece of linen doesn't require a lot of skill and the results won't look amateur.

Dried flowers

If you have a love of nature and enjoy having bouquets of flowers around the home, then adding them to your walls can add textural interest. You can produce really beautiful results by drying flowers, leaves or seedheads with architectural shapes or with lots of delicate detail, or by pressing them in sheets of paper between heavy books and then framing them.

Fabric

Fabric is a lovely material to frame, whether it's a vintage textile you have sourced, a tea (dish) towel or tote bag. Material is a beautiful thing to display because it carries its own unique markings and texture.

Enhancing Your Zone /
The Holistic Home

In recent years a new focus within interior design has emerged which eschews a consumer-driven climate to focus on the considered home which enhances well-being while also being less harmful to the environment. Living in balance can be achieved in many ways, from a commitment to honest materials, to paying attention to the way our senses interact with environment. Your home is full of small rituals, from starting the day with deep breathing exercises, to setting the table for dinner and ushering in the evening. What these rituals have in common is the elevation of daily living, and a recognition of that which nurtures us.

A happy home is so much more than the look of the space. Thinking holistically about the home involves considering all five of our senses, and how we fully interact with a space should not be overlooked or replaced with visual saturation. How things feel, how they smell, how they nourish and sound – all these impact our experience of home. In the same way that the simple act of opening a window will allow us to feel the breeze or hear birds singing, considered homes utilise all of the senses to ground us in our living environment.

Daily interactions with our physical space can feel incredibly different with the simplest of changes, from those that are good to touch, or where the noise landscape is planned to avoid discord, through to ones which provide an inviting space to cook and eat.

Having plants in a space not only calms and connects us to nature but will also purify the air that we breathe. Smell is perhaps the sense most connected to our memory. Particular notes can evoke whole worlds of association, and choosing scents for the home that make you feel cheerful, cosy, at rest or enlivened is a perfect way of enhancing your daily routine. Home fragrance doesn't need to be a luxury item. If you know the fragrance notes you like it is easy to create your own blend of essential oils for burning or mixing with almond oil to create a reed diffuser.

As we all become more aware of climate crisis, the holistic approach to considered living becomes increasingly driven by demand for products that are less wasteful and built to last longer. From LED circuits to the glass bottles we use to store natural cleaning products, there is now a host of ways we can begin to reduce the impact our homes have on the environment. We are becoming far more conscious as consumers, aware of the devastating effects of fast fashion, and this filters through to interiors too. While I am all in favour of the accessibility afforded by high-street designs, buying an item on flirtation because you are attracted by the price is toxic to our planet. Before purchasing an item for the home, say a cheap side table, consider its footprint, the multiple materials used to create it. If you will keep it for a long time, it's a great investment, but if you can picture it in landfill, it's time to move past it.

From building materials, surfaces and fabrics, to paint and even tools, or wood taken from sustainable sources, there are now so many options for creating a home with sustainability at its heart. These days the design options are impressive, whether you want a terrazzo surface made from recycled plastic or an alternative to wood-burning stoves, eco-design has you covered. If you are wanting to build sustainability into your decorating, then you will want to use eco-conscious paint brands. With paint contributing huge toxicity to the environment, water-based natural pigments that are made with lower VOCs (volatile organic compounds) are a no-brainer, but there are other paint brands you can research who do more.

Biophilia

I would like to end our conversation by drawing attention to something which is inextricably linked to the modern holistic home - biophilia. Taking on many of the aspects discussed on pages 174–176, biophilia is defined as our innate connection to nature, and it has guided much new thought within interior design over the last decade. Focusing on the essentials of nature that help us to flourish, biophilia answers many of our modern needs and desires. It may be concerned with the restorative stimulus of natural light, our perception of movement - be that moving leaves and shifting shadows of a view from a window or cloud movement glimpsed through sky lights - or the sensory pitter patter of rain outside. Being able to see the connection between our homes and nature is proven to be both stimulating and life-enhancing.

Bringing the outside in is an important aspect of new thinking on mindful living, with proven strategies that benefit both physical health and emotional state. It can include adding plants to a windowsill or using natural materials for furniture and flooring to support an interior that feels restful. Living within conditions that connect us to nature - be they rooms with wooden cladding or spaces that mimic the motifs of nature in surface materials or with cotton and wool textiles - helps us to feel grounded. According to studies into biophilic design, these connections physically relax us, lowering blood pressure and heart rate.

It may seem logical that things that are growing, plants for example, are more likely to centre us in nature. However, indirect references such as honeycomb-shaped tiles, fractural patterned textiles, prints of nature and artificial reproductions of plants all have centring properties that make us feel better. If you are a collector, biophilia could mean bringing in treasures from nature; responsibly sourced vintage entomology, shells, coral, feathers and precious stone. Nature doesn't have hard lines so using circles can be an interesting way of incorporating its motifs. We should all be able to bring more nature into our lives, even in small ways, which will be beneficial to both our happiness and balance.

Drying flowers and grasses is a really effective way of bringing biophilic principles into the home. Both wreaths and arrangements in vases give focus to the myriad of nature's intricacy. The architectural structures, or fragile beauty, of nature's skeletal delicacy can be witnessed in the subtle gesture of the tilt of a dried stem or of movement on small fronds atop a dried flower.

Design and Ecology with Lizzie Ruinard

Lizzie Ruinard runs London-based architecture practice neighbourhood studio, which is a founding member of the Dalston Architecture Collective, has been shortlisted for many industry architecture awards and has been featured by Houzz in their best design category. Lizzie has a passion for creating builds and fits with ecology at their centre, in sympathy with their surroundings. She has worked on wide-ranging briefs from residential projects and schools to commercial spaces that have featured in *Vogue* and she has appeared on the television series *Grand Designs*.

On the easiest points to focus on to create a sustainable home

Making sustainable design a key part of the approach from the concept stage is integral to an eco-focused project. Generally, this involves minimising the use of concrete, or other materials that contribute to the embodied carbon footprint, and maximising the use of natural alternatives, for example hempcrete, flax and cork, which absorb carbon dioxide.

On ways of making ecological choices without knocking down walls

If making smaller alterations to the home, I would suggest installing a smart meter, solar panels (if space allows), using LED light bulbs, water-based eco paint and making sure your house is as insulated and draughtproof as possible.

One way of making an old property more energy efficient is to look into your draught exclusion. This can be addressed fairly easily by adding brushes or seals to the gaps below existing doors, filling the tiny spaces around old windows which have warped over time and making sure you can close your chimney flue when a fire isn't burning.

On the most impressive eco material for the home

Hemp. This plant has the ability to absorb large amounts of carbon dioxide, improve air quality and modulate thermal performance. It is a fast-growing crop that can be processed and manufactured into a wide variety of building materials, from bricks to wall boards and plasters, alongside smaller interior uses, from table mats and ottomans to plant pots. Another impressive feature of this material is that all parts of the plant can be used.

On innovations which reduce waste in the home

There are some great smart meters which put the consumer in control of tracking and managing their energy use. Renewable heat technologies are coming in which will offer more energy-efficient alternatives to the traditional boiler, but these will rely on a well-insulated property in order to function properly.

On favourite ways to incorporate biophilia

I take a human-centred approach to the environment and try to create a connection between the internal and external spaces through the careful positioning of openings which capture views and light, bringing nature into the home. I always try to use natural finishes within a building as they create very grounding spaces which offer both tactile and visual enjoyment.

On where a renovator should focus insulation considerations, particularly in older period properties

I would advise taking a 'fabric first' approach. This essentially means maximising the performance of the existing building components while maintaining 'breathability'. Buildings that were created pre-inter-war were not designed to keep water out completely, but rather modulate moisture levels using materials which allowed the building to 'breathe' and as such avoid dampness and decay. Generally old buildings perform very well if alterations to the existing fabric respect this ethos.

Adding breathable insulation, such as sheep's wool, hemp, flax or cork, is one of the principle methods of improving thermal performance. The easiest places to do this are in the attic or below a suspended timber ground floor, where you can lift the boards and drape insulation between them with minimal impact on the existing house.

About the Author

Ruth Matthews is an interiors blogger and consultant, stylist and photographer based in London. In 2013, she started her blog Design Soda to document her design journey creating a beautiful, small space on a tight budget. Nine years later, she is now the proud owner of a house, but her MO remains the same – to make an interesting and stylish home without breaking the bank.

Acknowledgements

They say that it takes a village to raise a child. It's similar with a book. I would like to thank my lovely commissioning editor at Hardie Grant, Kate Burkett, who approached me with the original idea and helped me realise my exacting vision and dream of writing a book. Also, Nikki Ellis, the designer, and Sarah Hogan, who photographed my home so beautifully. Having chosen every image for the book, I am hugely grateful to everyone who agreed to inclusion – this wouldn't have been the same book without you! I am also hugely grateful to my expert contributors Joa Studholme, Lizzie Evans and Lizzie Ruinard, who answered all of my questions with insight and aplomb, providing such wonderful tips for readers.

On a personal note, the village of all my friends and family. Dan, my husband of 13 years, the wisest and most grounded person I know, also my cheerleader in life. Ted, my son, whose arrival was the catalyst for a career in interiors and who is my every joy. My mum, for offering last-minute childcare to get me past the line, and for being such a wonderful human. Special mention to Dinah the cat, who contributed nothing, but is a good photo prop and kept me company throughout. My wide circle of friends who make me the luckiest of people, particularly those who are closest – Kathryn, Joanna, Alex and Tamla, who were sounding boards with erudite suggestions throughout writing, love you all.

And of course, what is a book without a reader? Thank you to those who have followed my blog Design Soda since it first launched in 2013, and those who have joined me via Instagram along the way. I love having conversations with you daily. Since I started blogging, I have met, and been inspired by, numerous people I now count as friends, but chief amongst them: Melanie Lissack, Cate St Hill and Bianca Hall.

Credits

Every reasonable effort has been made to acknowledge the copyright of images in this volume. Any errors or omissions that may have occurred are inadvertent and will be corrected in subsequent editions provided notification is sent in writing to the publisher.

Page 2: Photograph by Sarah Hogan.

Page 7: Cate St Hill, @catesthill.

Page 8 (top): Karen Knox – Making Spaces.

Page 8 (bottom): Trilby Road. Design by 2LG Studio. Photograph by Megan Taylor.

Pages 9 and 10: Photographs by Sarah Hogan.

Page 13: Smash Hits. Design by 2LG Studio. Photograph by Megan Taylor.

Page 14: Photography and styling by Theo-Bert Pot, @theobert_pot.

Page 17: Anki Wijnen, @zilverblauw

Page 18: Cate St Hill, @catesthill.

Page 21: Design by A NEW DAY Interiors. Photograph by Anna Stathaki, @annastathakiphoto.

Page 23: Cate St Hill, @catesthil

Page 25: Photography and styling by Theo-Bert Pot, @theobert_pot.

Page 26: Home of Kathryn Bristow, Interior Stylist and Retail Specialist. Photograph by Kasia Fiszer.

Page 29: Photograph by Cathy Pyle, @cathy.pyle.

Page 30: Design by A NEW DAY Interiors. Photograph by Anna Stathaki, @annastathakiphoto.

Pages 32–33: Interior Design: Emilie Fournet Interiors. Photograph by Kasia Fiszer.

Page 35: Jess Hurrell, Interior Stylist @gold_is_a_neutral. Photograph by Kasia Fiszer.

Page 36: Photos: Helenio Barbetta/Living Inside. Styling by Laura Mauceri.

Page 39: Photography and styling by Theo-Bert Pot, @theobert_pot.

Pages 40–41: Trellik Design Studio 'French+Tye'.

Page 43 Design by Hello Flora @helloflorauk.

Page 45: Styling by Kay Prestney. Photograph by Cathy Pyle, @cathy.pyle.

Pages 46–47: Justin Coakley, @design_at_nineteen.

Page 48–49: Casa Horta. Photograph by José Hevia.

Pages 50–51: Kinveachy Gardens. Homeowner: Emily Mayne of www.somedaydesigns.co.uk Photograph by Anna Stathaki, @annastathakiphoto.

Pages 52–53 and 54: Photographs by Sarah Hogan.

Page 57: Grillo Designs. Photograph by Kasia Fiszer.

Page 59: Granville Park. Design by 2LG Studio. Photograph by Megan Taylor.

Pages 60–61: Studio Ben Allen. Photographs by 'French+Tye'.

Page 63: Photograph by Sarah Hogan.

Page 64: Photograph by Cathy Pyle, @cathy.pyle.

Pages 66–67: Patricia Goijens, @patriciagoijens.

Pages 69 and 71: Ruth Matthews, @Design_Soda_Ruthie.

Pages 74–75: Design by 2LG Studio. Photograph by Megan Taylor.

Page 77: Jonas Ingerstedt Photography @jonasingerstedtphotography.

Page 78: Susanna Hawkins.

Page 81: Photography and styling: Carole Poirot, @carole.poirot.

Page 82: Sandra Baker @the_idle_hands.

Index

Published in 2022 by Hardie Grant Books,
an imprint of Hardie Grant Publishing

Hardie Grant Books (London)
5th & 6th Floors
52–54 Southwark Street
London SE1 1UN

Hardie Grant Books (Melbourne)
Building 1, 658 Church Street
Richmond, Victoria 3121
hardiegrantbooks.com

British Library Cataloguing-in-Publication Data. A catalogue
record for this book is available from the British Library.

Own Your Zone

ISBN: 978-178488-559-5

10 9 8 7 6 5 4 3 2 1

Acting Publishing Director: Emma Hopkin
Publishing Director: Kajal Mistry
Commissioning Editor: Kate Burkett
Copy Editor: Gillian Haslam
Proofread: Lucy York
Design: Nikki Ellis
Picture Researcher: Katie Horwich
Photography on pages 2, 9, 10, 52, 53, 54, 63, 97, 103, 111, 127, 139,
145, 158, 163, 169 and 170: Sarah Hogan
Photography Assistant: Sam Peter Reeves
Production Controller: Lisa Fiske

Colour reproduction by p2d
Printed and bound in China by Leo Paper Products Ltd.